EDUCATION AND LIBERTY

The Role of the Schools in a Modern Democracy

EDUCATION
and LIBERTY

The Role of the Schools in
a Modern Democracy

JAMES BRYANT CONANT

HARVARD UNIVERSITY PRESS

Cambridge, Massachusetts

1956

*This book is based on Lectures delivered at
the University of Virginia under the
Page-Barbour Foundation on
February 12, 13, 14, 1952.*

PREFACE

FOR SOME YEARS I have had in mind attempting a comparison of secondary education in the United States with that in several nations of the British Commonwealth. It seemed to me that a study of methods of educating the youth of Australia and New Zealand might throw light on some of the problems facing us in the United States, for these countries, like our own, have developed educational traditions that stem from England and Scotland in the seventeenth and eighteenth centuries. A trip to the Antipodes in July and August 1951, made possible by the generosity of the Carnegie Corporation, gave me an opportunity to talk with a number of educators in Australia and New Zealand. The invitation to give the Page-Barbour Lectures at the University of Virginia seemed to provide an appropriate occasion for a review of my findings in relation to a discussion of education and liberty. For I intended to retraverse some of the ground which the Father of the University first explored in his writings on education. Thomas Jefferson's works might be an old story to a Virginia audience, but to reread what he wrote about education and liberty is to renew one's faith in the lasting significance of what has been accomplished on the North American continent in the last one hundred and fifty years.

In a letter to George Washington in 1786, Jefferson wrote, "It is an axiom in my mind that our liberty can never be safe but in the hands of the people themselves, and that, too, of the people with a certain degree of instruction." [1] This sentence I took as my text for my three lectures. Starting with Jefferson's axiom, which has become an assumption in all modern democracies, it is important to examine what in the mid-twentieth century is the "degree of instruction" that should be provided for *all* our youth in order that in the future our liberty may be safe in the hands of the people.

Although it may have been presumptuous for one from an erstwhile stronghold of Federalism — the college of the Adamses — to quote Jefferson to an audience in Virginia, I began the lectures by reading his well-known statement summing up the double duties that have faced the schools of this democracy from his time to the present. Looking back at what he had accomplished and on what he had attempted in 1779, he wrote to John Adams in 1813 as follows:

"At the first session of our Legislature after the Declaration of Independence, we passed a law abolishing entails. And this was followed by one abolishing the privilege of primogeniture, and dividing the lands of intestates equally among all their children, or other representatives. These laws, drawn by myself, laid the axe to the root of pseudo-aristocracy. And had another, which I proposed, been adopted by the legislature, our work would have been complete. It was a bill for the more general diffusion of learning. This proposed to divide every county into wards of five or six miles square, like your townships, to establish in each ward a free school for reading, writing and common arithmetic, to provide for the annual selection of the best subjects [that is, pupils] from these schools, who might receive at the public expense a higher degree of education at a district school and from these district schools to select a certain number of the most promising subjects, to be completed at a university where all the useful

---

[1] Roy J. Honeywell, *The Educational Work of Thomas Jefferson* (Harvard University Press, 1931), p. 13.

sciences should be taught. Worth and genius would thus have
been sought out from every condition of life, and completely
prepared by education for defeating the competition of
wealth and birth for public trusts." [2]

The general diffusion of learning and the complete education of men of "worth and genius" are the twofold objectives
of the free schools of the United States. How in the twentieth
century may these objectives be best achieved? This is the
question I raised in the three Page-Barbour Lectures which I
had the honor of presenting at the university of Thomas
Jefferson.

These lectures, somewhat revised and expanded by the
addition of notes (to be found in the back of the book), comprise this volume. The last half of the third lecture, dealing
with the relation of private and public schools, formed the
basis of an address I delivered at a meeting of the American
Association of School Administrators in Boston on April 7,
1952. It was reprinted in the *Saturday Review* and in the
Harvard *Alumni Bulletin* and has been the subject of considerable discussion, in part based on misleading headlines in
the daily press. I have therefore endeavored by some modifi-
cations and ample notes to clarify my position on one of the
great issues now facing the American public, namely, whether
we are to support an expansion of private schools through the
use of public funds.[3]

The first chapter of this book presents a comparison of
British and American education; the next considers that special American invention, the four-year liberal arts college and
its influence on secondary education; the third and last chapter outlines some of the problems we now face in the United
States and suggests certain answers; it likewise emphasizes
the unique nature of the comprehensive public high school

---

[2] *Ibid.*, pp. 8–9.
[3] The substance of Chapter III appears in *The Virginia Quarterly Review*,
Vol. 28, No. 4 (Autumn 1952), pp. 500–517.

and considers some of the criticisms currently directed against it.

My inquiry has been focused on the education of the adolescent: for the nature of the schools and colleges best suited to serve a modern democracy by providing instruction to boys and girls from 12 to 20 is still a matter of debate. And this debate will be intensified by changes in the school population that will soon be upon us. The birth rate in the thirties was low; as a consequence we have somewhat fewer boys and girls of college age today than a decade earlier. But the birth rate in the forties was high and has stayed high to the present moment. There are something like 50 per cent more children under 8 years of age than there are between 10 and 18. Whether the birth rate will once again recede is an interesting question but one of secondary importance, for whether it does or not, we are now faced with the fact that the elementary schools already have to cope with a greatly increased number of pupils; we are certain that this bulge in the student population is at least ten years wide.

So far only the elementary schools have been affected by this wave of pupils. There can be no argument about what should be done in regard to elementary education. The basic pattern throughout the English-speaking nations was firmly set many years ago. No one is going to question today the necessity for providing full-time education for all American children from the age of about 5 to 15. Having once decided to abolish illiteracy, no modern democracy is going to give up universal schooling, at least for children.

Without in the least minimizing the significance of elementary education, I suggest that our most serious problems will arise when the secondary schools begin to feel the impact of the increased birth rate of the forties and the fifties. For free secondary education on a large scale is a product of this century; the pattern is by no means the same in all the English-speaking countries. Indeed, it is quite different in the United States from that which has developed in any other nation.

As everyone is well aware, there is today an increased critical discussion of the role of the high schools in our American democracy. For many decades their aims and their methods have been subject to constant scrutiny, not only by professionals, but also by parents and citizens. This has been an important feature of their development. The local communities in this country have shaped their schools far more than in any other nation. That this is so is one of the significant aspects of our American pattern of tax-supported education. Through the device of community responsibility we have avoided to a large degree the danger of a state-imposed uniformity. Our multitude of local schools provides a great diversity while each one aims at being a center for developing a spirit of democratic coöperation.

The characteristic pattern of public education in this country has evolved during the last three quarters of a century. To my mind, it has provided a great engine of democracy which has served this nation of many creeds. Without it I doubt whether so many different national cultures brought by the nineteenth-century migrations could have found a common basis of understanding. I believe its work is nowhere near completed. Admittedly many of our public schools fall far short of the ideal. Therefore the problem is: Shall we improve the schools or change the pattern? There are powerful persons who urge the latter course. It is for the American people to decide, but the nature of the problem needs to be understood. With the hope that a comparative study may be of value in this connection, these lectures were first written and are now prepared for publication.

I take this opportunity of recording my indebtedness to the University of Virginia for the invitation to be the Page-Barbour Lecturer, and my gratitude for the hospitality of my entertainment and the generous reception of my lectures by the audiences assembled.

JAMES B. CONANT

Cambridge, Massachusetts
July 15, 1952

CONTENTS

I

THE ANGLO-SAXON TRADITION

II

III

EDUCATION AND LIBERTY

The Role of the Schools in a Modern Democracy

❧ I ❧

THE ANGLO-SAXON
TRADITION

IN THIS CHAPTER I propose to examine the present
status of secondary education in four British countries and the
United States. I have chosen England, Scotland, Australia,
and New Zealand; I have omitted Canada because of the
complications of the bilingual culture of sections of that country and the fact that the education there presents a pattern
not entirely British. In this review, as in the other chapters, I
have had in mind the reader who has no professional connection with education. This is not a scholarly treatise for teachers or school administrators but an attempt to clarify certain
educational problems that must concern every responsible
citizen. For the future of our public schools will be determined by the policies set by the American people.

I am hoping that some readers may find that educational
questions not only appeal to their sense of duty as citizens,
but arouse intellectual curiosity as well. For once you stop
talking about schools primarily in terms of either pedagogy
or taxes and consider the relation of a society to its youth in
general terms, you enter an exciting area. Education must be
regarded as a social process; it is related in each country to
the current political scene, the social history of the nation, and
the national ideals. Thus a comparative study of education

must take one far beyond the confines of the school. Even in such a relatively superficial survey as that presented in this volume, it will become evident that the social behavior characteristic of a people is more significant in determining the nature of the schools than the acceptance of any particular philosophy of education.

One word of warning at the outset: I do not believe that educational practices are an exportable commodity. I fear the contrary assumption has been implied to some extent in our dealings with Germany and Japan since the close of World War II. At times in our own history, attempts to import a British or European concept have done more harm than good. It is extremely difficult to say what is a good educational procedure except in terms of a particular society; a school cannot be separated from the context of the families that it serves nor from the over-all social framework in which the pupils will probably function as adults. With these thoughts in mind, the reports presented in this chapter will be taken, I hope, as stimuli for our own thinking in the United States rather than as foreign patterns to be either copied or condemned.

Let us start with a quick over-all survey of the patterns of secondary education in the five countries under consideration — England, Scotland, Australia, New Zealand, and the United States. If one considers only the number of adolescents attending school full time, the difference between the United States on the one hand and the British countries on the other is both striking and significant. *The uniqueness of the American pattern can be summed up in two sentences. In the United States, less than a third of the boys and girls 16 to 17 years of age are* not *attending school. In the four British countries, less than a third of the same age group are attending school.* This contrast is best brought out by noting the age at which the youth of each nation terminates full-time education. Needless to say, in no one of the countries is there a final year beyond which no one may continue full-time education. Rather, in each case a certain percentage of the boys and girls over 14 drop out of school each year. These percentages form a characteristic pattern when arranged by age groups (that is, 13-year-olds, 14-year-olds, and so on). While the pattern has changed markedly in each country over the decades and is still changing, as we shall see, there are no sharp fluctuations from year to year. Hence a comparison reveals at once basic information about the education of adolescents in each of the five countries.

TABLE 1

Educational Patterns for Adolescents in Four British Countries and the United States

Percentage of Age Group (Boys and Girls) in Full-Time Education as of Beginning of the School Year, 1950[1]

Age Group	England	Scotland	Australia *			New Zealand	U.S.A.†
			(1)	(2)	(3)		
13	98+	98+	98+	98+	96	98+	95
14	98+	95	69	95	63	98	93
15	31	37	42	38	35	60	88
16	16	14	22	18	18	33	76
17‡	7.5	9	11	14	12	15	61

* (1) South Australia, (2) New South Wales, (3) Victoria.
† Figures are for 1940.
‡ A considerable number of the students in the Universities are 17–18 and are included except in the case of England and New Zealand.

Table 1 brings out clearly the special position of the United States in regard to the number of adolescents pursuing a lengthy educational course.[1] Consider, for example, the first line, the figures for the age group 13 (that is, all the boys and girls over 13 and under 14 on the date for which the statistics are valid). It is clear that, with the exception of one of the three Australian states studied, essentially all the youth of all

[1] The numbers refer to the notes beginning on page 91.

the countries are attending school on a full-time basis up to the age of at least 14. Indeed, with the exception of two Australian states, the same statement is true in regard to education up to the age of 15. It is in the next age group — 15 — that significant differences occur; even more striking are the differences between the figures representing the percentage of the age group 16 attending school in the different countries.

The percentage in New Zealand places this country on the borderline of my generalization. And if the reader will consider the comparison for the age group 15 he will notice that the New Zealand pattern is at this point similar to that of the United States rather than the three other British countries. This is no irrelevant accident but the consequence of a very deliberate change in the nature of secondary education in New Zealand some ten years ago which will be considered later.

If the contrast were confined to Great Britain and the United States, the difference might be said to reflect dissimilarities between an old civilization and a pioneering nation. But this easy generalization crumbles before the statistics for Australia and New Zealand. Newness alone will not account for the uniqueness of the American pattern; nor will the tide of opinion that set in about 1905 and resulted in social welfare legislation, particularly in the last twenty years. Australia and New Zealand have gone far in this direction and have had labor party governments off and on for more than a generation. Yet their educational pattern resembles that of the mother country more than that of the United States.

There is probably no one answer to the question, why is our American pattern so different? In the next chapter I shall consider one reason — the influence of the American four-year liberal arts college which has no equivalent in other lands. Indeed, a comparison of the college and university enrollment in the five countries emphasizes even more the special position of the United States. Something like 20 per cent of the American youth of college age attend a college or university full time for at least a year, while the maximum figure in any other English-speaking nation is not over 7 per cent. But to contrast the American college with the British university before considering the secondary schools in each country would be to put the cart before the horse. In each nation the entire educational system has developed as part of the social history of the country.

ENGLAND

Logically, any review of British secondary education should start with England. Yet there are difficulties in the undertaking, for the English scene is now in a process of transition; the years ahead, not the present status, are perhaps more germane to a comparative study of secondary education.[2] Indeed, a Scottish university administrator remarked to me not long ago that until the Act of 1944 England never had an educational system. Whether that be a neighborly exaggeration or not, the Minister of Education for England and Wales wrote in 1946: "For the first time in the history of this country genuine secondary education is to be provided for all children over eleven . . . [as a consequence of the Act of 1944] . . . Secondary education is to be the right of all, and no longer the privilege of a few."[3]

Sir John Maud, Permanent Secretary, Ministry of Education for England and Wales, has written as follows:

In 1851 education was the part of English life of which Englishmen had least reason to be proud (I say nothing of Scotland in what follows). Society consisted of two "nations," one of which could afford to pay for its education and one which could not; and of formal education neither nation had much opportunity.

As for the "rich" nation, Oxford and Cambridge Universities were open only to professing members of the Church of England, and elsewhere in England there were practically no opportunities of university education except in London, Durham and Manchester. . . Public Schools (in the modern sense) [not in the American sense] were few in number, barbaric in character and confined to boys. . . With a few exceptions . . . the endowed grammar schools had not recovered from a century of decay; the Dissenting Academies were on the wane.

As for the "poor" nation, no schooling at all would have been available except for the missionary zeal of hotly competitive religious denominations. . .

In so far as the state felt concern for education, the concern was akin to that felt for the destitute and expressed in the poor law and the workhouse. Of public authorities for education, there was none to represent any local community. . .

During the twenty years that followed 1850 no politician of any party would risk offending either Anglicans or Dissenters by even proposing an Education Bill. . .

By 1870 the two nations were even further apart, in educational opportunity, than they had been in 1850. . . By the end of the century the gap was perhaps still wider, but the opportunities of each nation had been immensely improved. Literacy was brought within the reach of all children of the labouring poor — by . . . [the] Education Act of 1870. . . .

[In 1899] the two kinds of [elementary] schools — voluntary and publicly provided — were brought at last into a coherent relationship under a single local authority. . . But, between the Education Acts of 1902 and 1918, the most important change in education itself was the creation and development of the municipal secondary school. From now onwards, increasing numbers of children in the "poor" nation could obtain secondary education. . .

School education in the England and Wales of 1951 is still the education of two "nations," one fee-paying and one not. . . . Within the latter nation there are still two "tribes," the one at grammar schools and the other not. . . The two tribes will become one only when secondary education becomes generally and palpably available, not only in the grammar schools, but in secondary modern, secondary technical, bilateral, multilateral, or comprehensive schools, and when these latter schools are properly housed and staffed, and have become (as many modern schools have in fact already become) as first-rate in their own way as the best grammar schools have long been in theirs.[4]

In short, a system of free secondary education is still in the initial stages of development in England. The pattern ten or twenty years from now will be different from the present. It is with this reservation in mind that the figures in Table 1 must be compared with those of other nations. The Act of 1944 provided that the Minister of Education should raise the school-leaving age to 16 as soon as practical. The difficulties of the postwar period and the increasing international tension of the 1950's have made it necessary to postpone this further expansion of free secondary education much longer than originally anticipated. When this takes place, essentially 100 per cent of the youth 15–16 years of age will be enrolled in full-time education (the corresponding figure for the United States is, in 1952, about 95 per cent). The percentage of this group enrolled in England today, it is important to note, is twice that of five years earlier. That this expansion was accomplished in a period of almost unprecedented strain makes it an event of outstanding significance in the educational history of the English-speaking peoples.

An American observer examining English education must be constantly on guard to avoid misinterpreting what seem to be familiar words. The use of the words "public schools" in England to denote certain types of private schools is an obvious example. "Secondary education" is also a phrase that has been used somewhat differently in England than in the United States. Indeed, the meaning of this phrase has only recently undergone a change. Thus the Minister of Education for England and Wales wrote as follows in 1946:

There has been some confusion about the meaning of the phrase "secondary education for all." Until 1944 a "Secondary School" meant a particular sort of school to which only a small proportion of the population could aspire, one which had better qualified and better paid staff, smaller classes, and more attractive premises and amenities than most of the other schools in its neighborhood. It was attended by some of the ablest pupils selected by a highly competitive examination, and by a certain number of other pupils of varying abilities whose parents could afford to pay fees. This sort of secondary school will still remain, doing its own special job, and it will be at the service of all children for whom its educational provision is considered to be the most suitable. But it is now only one type of secondary school, to which pupils with particular leanings and aptitudes will go. In future there will be various types of secondary schools and various courses within secondary schools, which will offer children an education specially suited to their particular needs. All these schools will have the advantages and the amenities hitherto exclusively associated with the limited number of schools called secondary schools up to 1944.[5]

As matters stand in 1952, something like 71 per cent of the boys and girls 11 to 12 years of age in England start to follow nonacademic courses in publicly-maintained schools; about 6 per cent of these subsequently transfer to other schools, 4.5 per cent to technical courses and 1.5 per cent to academic courses. About 25 per cent of the same age group start courses of study which might eventually lead to a university; of these, about 18 per cent are in publicly maintained or aided "Grammar Schools" and another 6 or 7 per cent in independent schools.[6] The opportunities for pursuing an orthodox academic course are limited to those who attend an independent school which charges a fee (in this class fall the famous English "Public Schools" which are in fact private) and the Grammar Schools which are wholly or in part maintained at public expense.[7] There are at present more applicants for the Grammar Schools than there are places; the decision as to which children are admitted is made by the local education authorities on the basis of examinations. Thus a combination of the desire of parents and the judgment of examiners results in an almost irrevocable decision as to a child's future at age 11+. Transfer from one type of school to another is still possible but not frequent.

Now for the well-to-do and professional classes in England

there is nothing unusual about this situation. They are accustomed to sending their boys to private schools preparing for the "Public Schools" at this age. But to have the entrance into a tax-supported free school subject to this sort of early determination is another story. Families with ambitions for their sons but insufficient money to pay for a private boarding school education have in some cases protested.[8] In some localities educational opportunities once offered by a Grammar School for a relatively small fee are now open to all without a fee, but on a competitive basis. This may mean the exclusion of some children from what is almost the only road within their sight leading to a university.

The question is being asked in England, is 11+ too early an age to decide who is to receive a university education and who is not? The examination of this question places some recurrent American problems in a new light. If the future university graduate is to be a learned man in the sense that the nineteenth century used these words, he must start his directed education at 11 or 12. Certainly this is true if he is to complete his formal training by 21 or 22. And this is the aim throughout the British Commonwealth. If a boy or girl is to enter a university with a good grasp of two foreign languages, the study of languages almost has to be started early. If the old-fashioned secondary school curriculum of six years of Latin and four or five years of Greek, French, or German is adhered to, the course can hardly be less than six years in length. Indeed, the more you insist that the future professional student must have special knowledge and skills on entering a university, the earlier you force the decision as to whether or not a child eventually is to go to college. This fact is all too often dodged in the discussion of the inadequacies of American secondary schools.

In free schools the social compulsion, the family pressures that pertain to private schools are to a considerable degree absent. In free schools only the very gifted boy or girl is willing at age 12 to begin the kind of intensive study required if two languages, arithmetic, algebra and geometry as well as English grammar and literature are to be studied intensively for six years. Therefore, if there is not to be a high percentage of failures each year in these free schools, there must be a rigorous selection at the start by the public authorities.

The contrast of the English pattern with that typical of the United States will be evident to most readers. Only in the large cities and a relatively few towns are there publicly supported American secondary schools at all parallel to the English Grammar Schools.[9] The more usual situation is a comprehensive high school (often divided into a junior and senior high school). Within this school there may be — and to my mind there should be — different courses, some leading to a university, others more vocational in nature. But before discussing further this rather special product of American democracy — the comprehensive high school — let us examine the secondary school in three other countries.

SCOTLAND

England and Scotland have been one nation with one Parliament since 1707. But the history of education has taken quite different courses north and south of the Tweed.[10] This is reflected by a long series of separate Parliamentary enactments affecting primary and secondary schools. The Minister of Education who answers questions in the House of Commons today is responsible only for the expenditure of money for schools in England and Wales. The Secretary of State for Scotland answers for Scottish education. The Scottish and English universities, on the other hand, all receive public monies from the same Universities Grants Committee.

Scotland takes pride in the antiquity of her tradition of free schools. In the famous *First Book of Discipline* of 1560, of which John Knox was the chief author, the necessity for a system of schools and colleges is set forth. "Seeing that God hath determined that His Church here on earth shall be taught not by angels but by men . . ." the *Book of Discipline* states, it is necessary that the Government of Scotland "be most careful for the virtuous education and godly upbringing of the youth of this realm." [11] Grammar schools and colleges were to be widespread and "the great schools called Universities shall be replenished with those apt for learning." Furthermore it was declared, "The rich and potent may not be permitted to suffer their children to spend their youth in vain idleness, as heretofore they have done. They must be exhorted, and by censure of the Church compelled, to dedicate their sons, by good exercise, to the profit of the Church and to the Commonwealth . . . Provision must be made for those that are poor, and are not able by themselves, nor by their friends, to be sustained at letters . . ." [12]

The Commonwealth envisioned by John Knox was a strict Presbyterian theocracy. Scottish history flowed turbulently around this ideal for several centuries. The educational ambitions set forth in the *Book of Discipline*, it is perhaps fair to say, remained largely an ideal. A parish school system was established by a series of acts in the seventeenth century but the instruction was chiefly elementary even as late as the nineteenth. However, Alexander Morgan states that the Scottish people "enjoyed better educational facilities than any other portion of the empire" because of the parish schools. [13] In the eighteenth century these schools had been supplemented by additional grammar schools in the cities and towards the end of the century by private academies. However, in the first half of the nineteenth century something like 20 per cent of the children were attending no school at all. A Parliamentary Act of 1872 vastly improved the situation; elementary education became universal but "it made no provision for secondary or higher class schools." The Acts of 1908 and 1918 may be said, perhaps, to represent the first large scale provision of secondary education at public expense.[14] Today in Scotland schooling is essentially universal to age 15, over a third of those 15 to 16 and 14 per cent of those 16 years of age are in school (as shown in Table 1).

But the influence of Scotland on Anglo-Saxon education is not to be measured by either these twentieth-century figures (meager by American standards) or by the slow steps by which John Knox's goal has finally been attained. During the eighteenth and nineteenth centuries there was free education even if largely elementary; there was an opportunity for some poor but very able scholars to go to the university. Furthermore, there were few private schools comparable to the great English "Public Schools." Of course, the educational aims of the *Book of Discipline* were enmeshed in the religious orthodoxy of the time, but with this exception they may be regarded as anticipating those eighteenth-century ideals so eloquently expressed by Thomas Jefferson. Like Virginia, Scotland has been the point of origin of educational doctrines that have spread to far distant lands.

AUSTRALIA

In the eighteenth century, Scotsmen were among those migrating to the colonies in North America; in the nineteenth, to colonies in the Antipodes. To Australia and New Zealand came also many from England, from Wales, and from Ireland. Therefore, in these nations of the Southern Hemisphere today we find a merging of the Scottish, the English, and the Catholic Irish traditions of education. The union has been markedly affected by the socio-economic conditions in these new countries; also in the last twenty-five years by the experience of the United States and even more by the world-wide emphasis on equality of opportunity in the century of the common man.

When we turn to Australia to study secondary education we are at once struck by an amazing fact. Or at least it was amazing to me when I first discovered it. Nowhere in the world today does the private Protestant school flourish as it does in several Australian states — this on a continent more recently settled than North America and in a society famous for its labor governments and its concern for social welfare.

The flourishing state of independent schools in southeastern Australia today is no new phenomenon. On the contrary, until the second decade of this century little progress had been made in providing tax-supported secondary schools. Indeed, the example of the private schools was one of the factors forcing the development of state-supported secondary education in Australia as has recently been the case in England. In the second half of the nineteenth century the tradition of the English Public School was transplanted to Australia. This transplantation was so successful that this type of school in Australia is in terms of the number of pupils involved far more important than in the mother country. I must therefore digress briefly to consider the development in England of these so-called Public Schools.

THE ENGLISH PUBLIC SCHOOL TRADITION

Before the Reformation, education in England and Scotland, as elsewhere in Christendom, was a function of the Church. However, private instruction for sons of the nobility and rich burghers of the Middle Ages was a supplement to, or a substitute for, the organized schools staffed by men in religious orders. The use of private tutors for the children of kings and nobles is so ancient that I would hesitate to date the source. In a sense, the independent private schools in any country today can claim to be carrying on this tradition of providing the wellborn with an education suitable for their future status. Perhaps to some the connection of a modern private school with an ancient princely tutor may seem remote, but the descent of such schools from the old Public Schools of England can be clearly traced. In Great Britain itself the institutions are there to prove it; such truly ancient foundations as Winchester, chartered in 1382 by William of Wykeham, and Eton, founded in 1446 by Henry VI, have had a continuous and for the most part glorious history.

One feature — the pre-Reformation idea of providing scholarships for those who would enter the service of the Church — has long since disappeared. John Rodgers in his *The Old Public Schools of England* (1938) has written: "The seventy scholars who were intended by William of Wykeham to proceed to his Oxford foundation, New College, and then to fill the gaps in the secular clergy caused by the Black Death, were all to be poor boys. But Winchester, like nearly every other public school, has departed from its original purpose, and scholars and commoners alike are recruited from the wealthy families of society. It is one of the paradoxes of English life that the public schools, which were intended to be charitable institutions for the poor, are anything but public, and are reserved almost exclusively for the comparatively rich." [15]

In the eighteenth century, Winchester, Eton, Rugby, and a number of other famous schools all connected with the Established Church served the orthodox aristocracy and upper professional groups; a number of private dissenting academies served another wealthy social circle. The latter have disappeared, but the nineteenth century saw a tremendous invigoration of the "Public Schools." Indeed, in the period 1830–1870 the public school tradition became so powerful that its influence was felt throughout the Anglo-Saxon world. Speaking of this period, Trevelyan in his *English Social History* writes:

It might have been supposed that the age of Reform and the approach of democracy would lead to the improvement and multiplication of endowed Grammar Schools by State action; in that case a common education would have been shared by the clever children of very various classes, as had been done in the Grammar Schools of Tudor and Stuart times with such excellent results. But in the Victorian era the Grammar Schools remained less important. . . The new fashion was all for the "Public School" modelled on the old ideals of Eton, Winchester and Harrow, of which Rugby became the great exemplar. . . The "middling orders of society" found in the reformed Public School the door of entrance for their sons into the "governing class." The old landed gentry, the professional men and the new industrialists were educated together, forming an enlarged and modernized aristocracy, sufficiently numerous to meet the various needs of government and of leadership in Victoria's England and Victoria's Empire.[16]

The English "Public School" of the last quarter of the nineteenth century and the first quarter of the twentieth provided both for those who were going to Oxford and Cambridge to complete their education and for those who were going directly into the management of industry or commerce or into public service. The schools were by no means exclusively university preparatory institutions. The same is true today in both England and Australia. This is primarily because the British universities are professional institutions; there is nowhere in the British picture the equivalent of the American liberal arts college. But of that I shall have much more to say in the next chapter.

SECONDARY EDUCATION IN AUSTRALIA

The persistence of the tradition of the English "Public Schools" which we have just considered explains the success of the private schools in the more important cities of Australia (Table 2). Yet the headmaster of one of these schools objected when I once said that the Australian independent school was "frankly modeled" on the "Public Schools" of England. He pointed out certain highly important differences

TABLE 2

The Dual System in Australia

Distribution of Students by Age Groups between
Tax-supported and Private Schools (1948)

Percentage of Total Age Group (Boys and Girls) Enrolled

Age Group	South Australia °		New South Wales		Victoria °		
	Tax Supported	Private †	Tax Supported	Private †	Tax Sup.	Prot.	Cath.
13	78	20	75	25	69	8	19
14	50	19	72	23	42	9	12
15	27	15	24	14	20	8	7
16	10	11	10	8	7.5	6	3.8

° It will be noticed that in South Australia there are as many students aged 16 enrolled in the private schools as in the tax-supported schools and in Victoria 50 per cent more attending the independent institutions than studying in the free schools.[17]
† Protestant and Catholic.

— differences that account in no small measure for the lasting success of the private schools in the southeastern part of Australia. The schools with few exceptions are located in the large metropolitan areas (Sydney, the capital of New South Wales; Melbourne, the capital of Victoria; Adelaide, the capital of South Australia); they are not primarily boarding schools but rather day schools with a nucleus of boarders. The tuition has consequently been kept relatively low and the range of income groups of the families patronizing them is fairly broad. In each capital city there is a group of more or less competing schools, each with church connections; there are Church of England schools, Methodist schools, Presbyterian schools, and Catholic schools. The latter fall in a special category and what I have to say about the independent schools refers only to the non-Catholic institutions.

Superficially the English and Australian Public School may differ, but in essential features they are the same. This fact my informant not only admitted but emphasized. To quote his own words, these essentials are:

(1) The schools are independent. The School Council [Board of Trustees] appoints and dismisses the headmaster, and the headmaster, his staff; many men stay on the staff of one school for at least three quarters of their professional lives; numbers can be limited, and boys selected, if desired. These factors tend to give a school character, tradition, continuity, which tend to be lacking in a state-controlled school.

(2) The school's aim, even more than academic attainments, is the development of an active and effective sense of moral and spiritual values, and the linking of these with the Christian religion from which those in charge of the school believe those values cannot be separated.

(3) The means towards realizing these aims should be practical — worship in Chapel, corporate life in houses, teams, cadet detachments, self-government by the prefect system — as well as the mental discipline of the class-room.[18]

I have no doubt that similar statements could be obtained from headmasters of many private schools in the United States, though we have the tradition of the secular private school as well as the church-connected school. A conference of the heads of all the independent non-Catholic schools in the English-speaking nations would, I feel sure, arrive at a fair measure of common agreement on many extracurricular matters and certainly would agree as to the importance of these matters. As to the content of the curriculum, however, the British and the Americans would for the most part have to agree to disagree. We should think the English and the

Australians far too orthodox and conservative in academic matters; they would think us too ready to water down the studies and run riot with new pedagogic methods. There would be exceptions, of course, but in the main the lines would be drawn as I have indicated.

The reasons for the cleavage are closely related to the vast difference between the degree-granting institutions in the British nations on the one hand and those in the United States on the other. For the purposes of the present comparison it is necessary only to note that the Australian private schools, like the English "Public School" and the English Grammar Schools, provide a curriculum to be found in the United States in only a few college preparatory schools. Yet in Australia as in England, the private school, it need be remembered, is not exclusively a university preparatory school but provides a terminal education for many of the sons of the well-to-do. Indeed, throughout the British Commonwealth (always excepting Canada) graduates of both private and tax-supported high schools more often than not enter industrial life, even in inherited positions of responsibility, without attending a university. This is difficult for Americans to understand, but of the first importance in comprehending the British scene.

When free secondary education began to expand in Australia as in the United States, the fact was recognized that there must be some separation of the pupils into different types of schools or at least different programs — one program which roughly paralleled the private school, others that were more practical. Only from the former could students enter the university; from the others they entered part-time technical colleges. The interesting fact, however, is that today in Australia students are dropping out in large numbers before they complete the course from the free schools, even the more academic high schools. On the other hand, the private non-Catholic schools keep a majority of their students until graduation. (See the figures for the Protestant schools in Victoria, Table 2, p. 16.)

The holding power of these schools is a highly important social phenomenon. It is not new, for since the revitalization of the English Public School one hundred and twenty-five years ago, it was assumed that the pupil should complete a fairly lengthy course. This assumption has become one of the mores of the families who patronize the private schools in Great Britain and Australia; this I am inclined to think is the prime factor in preventing boys and girls from leaving these schools. Another is the absence of pressure on these children to earn money to help out the family budget. In Australia, where there is a severe labor shortage, the boy or girl from a low-income family is severely tempted to leave school after 14 and add substantially to the family budget by taking a job. (This same factor operates in the United States in many sectors of society.) Still a third force that holds boys in private schools undoubtedly is the school spirit, the attractiveness of the extracurricular aspects of the private school. Indeed, one may speculate that these aspects of school life had to be developed to a considerable degree to hold the interest of the student to make up for a curriculum loaded heavily with "book learning."

Now, if the private schools' holding their pupils is one measure of their success, the question naturally arises, why shouldn't the tax-supported school be made equally attractive? If full-time education is a "good thing" for the boy or girl of a family who can afford to pay for a private school, why isn't it a "good thing" for the poor boy or girl as well? Consciously or unconsciously this question, when turned into an argument, has impelled the spread of tax-supported secondary schools in Australia, New Zealand, and in recent years in England too.

The argument just outlined can be supplemented by another based on the need of society for well-trained professional talent. Take the figures for any one of the Australian states and note that less than 10 per cent of the age group enter a university; then turn to Table 1 and you will see that this 10 per cent must be drawn from not over twice that number enrolled in school at ages 16 to 17. This number in turn is less than a quarter of the total number of potential students. In other words, as far as selecting the talented students is concerned, the selection process has largely taken place before 16; to a considerable degree it takes place, as in England, when the educational road forks still earlier, one branch leading to the university, the other to the nonprofessional vocations.[19]

Now, it can be argued, and many Americans would argue, that a better selection can be made for university work if a large percentage of an age group is available from which to select and if the selection is made at a relatively mature age (18 or even later). But this Jeffersonian argument for holding youth in school is not the usual one. The more common and more persuasive is the argument I have given earlier that directs attention to the advantages that come to all who pursue education on a full-time basis to age 17 or 18. This approach to public education has been the official viewpoint of the New Zealand government for some fifteen years. As a consequence, the New Zealand pattern now resembles the American rather than the Australian.

NEW ZEALAND

The Minister of Education of New Zealand, writing in 1939, said:

The structure of the New Zealand school system as originally laid down (and, indeed, of practically all the school systems of the world) was based on the principle of *selection*. An elementary education in the three R's was given to all the population but beyond that schooling had to be either bought by the well-to-do, or won, through scholarships by the specially brilliant. . . . The present Government was the first [in New Zealand] to recognize explicitly that continued education is no longer a special privilege for the well-to-do or the academically able, but a right to be claimed by all who want it to the fullest extent that the State can provide. Important consequences follow from the acceptance of this principle. It is not enough to provide more places in schools of the older academic type that were devised originally for the education of the gifted few. Schools that are to cater for the whole population must offer courses that are as rich and varied as are the needs and abilities of the children who enter them. . . . It was necessary to convert a school system, constructed originally on a basis of selection and privilege, to a truly democratic form where it can cater for the needs of the whole population over as long a period of their lives as is found possible and desirable.[20]

These words might have been written by a member of the Educational Policies Commission of the National Education Association of the United States which prepared in 1944 the book entitled *Education for All American Youth*.[21] In other words, I might have, with certain changes in phraseology, written them myself. Indeed, one hears it frequently stated that the New Zealand schools have been Americanized. Whether that is a good thing or not will depend largely on the point of view of the observer. An eminent Canadian educator who is disturbed by the North American tendency to think of schooling age 13 to 18 as a generalized preparation for life has written me that he is a "good deal less happy about the changes in New Zealand" than I am. However, that the educational pattern has been altered to some degree there can be no doubt. In terms of the per cent of boys and girls aged 15 and 16 enrolled in secondary school, the New Zealand picture now resembles that of the United States more than it does that of the other British nations (Table 1, p. 3). The changes of which the New Zealand Minister wrote, without doubt increased the holding power of the schools. At the same time, they present serious problems to the university in New Zealand with which the faculties are still wrestling [22] and which are reminiscent of similar problems in the United States.

Seventy-five years ago it was assumed throughout the English-speaking world that the basis for university work was a classical education. The Grammar Schools and the "Public Schools" in England set the standard. The agitation for the introduction of science, modern languages, and a study of English literature, while not new, was just beginning to gain momentum. In Australia and New Zealand, as in the mother country, the strict classical course for future university students was replaced years ago by a modernized version. But even this modernized version is still in most Australian states a narrowly confined and lengthy study of foreign languages, mathematics, and English, with physics and chemistry replacing one language for those who so desire. As in the English "Public School" and Grammar School, specialization begins young in Australia; what we Americans call general education is conspicuous by its absence.[23]

The objectives of the New Zealand reforms were the introduction of more flexibility into the curriculum so that a youth may postpone the decision to enter a university until nearer the end of his school course, the introduction of a "common core" of studies, and greater attention to such subjects as history, social studies, geography, fine arts, and music.[24] That most students find such a diversified curriculum more attractive than the older one tightly tied to a few subjects is clearly evident; that something has been gained in providing that "degree of instruction" required for preserving the liberties of the people, I for one feel certain. That something has been lost for the gifted boy who later becomes a professional leader seems at first sight obvious. Yet the experience in the United States may indicate that less is lost than those who believe in an old-fashioned secondary curriculum maintain. By the time an individual graduates from an American medical school or law school, the differences in secondary school preparation seem to have largely disappeared. But I must postpone further discussion of this topic until a later chapter.

The report on New Zealand would be incomplete without noting that there are in the country only a few Protestant private schools as compared to Australia, and their total enrollment is small. Only about 14 per cent of the total of those enrolled in primary education attend private schools, and even for the age group 16 the figure rises only to something like 17 per cent, while the corresponding figures for South Australia, New South Wales, and Victoria are 52 per cent, 44 per cent, and 57 per cent.[25] Why is the role of the private school so different in New Zealand and Australia? One is an exaggeration of the nineteenth-century English pattern, the other that of the Scottish. This fact suggests one possible explanation in terms of the relative number of Scotch and English immigrants in the two countries. This is related to the high percentage of Presbyterians in New Zealand. The preponderance of the Scotch in certain localities in New Zealand may be a partial answer. I suggest, however, that the more important factor is to be found by examining the distribution of the population in the two nations.

In spite of its enormous size and relatively few inhabitants, Australia is a highly urbanized country. Approximately 50 per cent of the population lives in the capital cities of the six states. Sydney and Melbourne are the second and third largest cities anywhere in the British Commonwealth, including England. As I have already pointed out, the independent schools are located in the cities. They flourish primarily as day schools, not as boarding schools. In New Zealand there are no large cities. With a population of about half the size of the largest Australian city, there are four rival commercial and cultural centers. There appears not to be the concentration of well-to-do people in any of these to support a group of Protestant day schools similar to those found in Australian cities. Notice I say a group, for in a country which has no established church and is the home of several sects, there must be several church-connected schools if the ideal of the English "Public School" is to be widely realized.[26]

THE UNITED STATES

I shall assume that the reader is far more familiar with secondary schools in the United States than in any other country. Therefore in a few paragraphs I shall sketch only the outlines of some aspects of American education, directing attention in particular to those aspects which are characteristic of the pattern that has evolved on this continent in the last fifty years.

The data already summarized in Table 1 emphasize the fact that only in the United States do more than two thirds of the adolescents attend school on a full-time basis. This characteristic pattern is the result of marked changes that occurred just after the turn of the century, as is shown by Table 3.[27]

A comparison with Table 1 shows that in regard to full-time attendance of adolescents, the situation in the other countries under review (except New Zealand) is similar to that which prevailed in the United States during the transition period more than forty years ago. I venture to underline the fact that for nearly half a century the American people have supported public secondary schools that enroll three times as large a fraction of the youth 16 years of age as *now* attend school in England, Scotland, or Australia.

The figures given in Tables 1 and 3 are over-all percentages for the entire United States. In some states a much higher percentage of young people attend secondary schools than the national average, in others, far fewer. For example, in 1940 in California and Utah the figures for the 16-year-old enrollment are as high as 91 per cent; in New York state the percentage of that age group enrolled full time is 88.1; in some other states the figure is as low as 49.1 (Kentucky).[28]

TABLE 3

The Change of the Secondary School Pattern in the United States

Percentage of Age Group Attending School

Year	Age Group				
	10–13	14	15	16	17
1890	80 †	*	*	*	*
1900	80 †	*	*	*	*
1910	88 †	81	68	51	35
1920	93	86	73	51	35
1930	97	93	85	66	48
1940	96	93	88	76	61
1950	99	95 *		71 *	

* The individual figures for the separate age groups are not available.
† The only age breakdown available is 10–14.

The same lack of uniformity would be found when it came to comparing the relative numbers in tax-supported and private schools. For the whole country in 1950 about 92 per cent of those attending secondary schools are in public schools, something like 6 per cent in church-connected schools and less than 2 per cent in other private schools. But in some states the relative proportion of private school pupils would be much higher, and like the fluctuation in total enrollment, there would be vast differences from community to community within certain states.[29]

Anyone attempting to describe the secondary schools of the United States in a few pages has an impossible task. The variations are so great from state to state because we do not have a national system; even within a single state they are as great as they are because strictly speaking we do not have a *system* of free state schools anywhere in the Union. The contrast with Australia is evident. In that nation, too, there are no national enactments about schools; education, as with us, is a matter for each state. But each state does have a unified system with a permanent government official at the head (a Director of Education) and a Minister of Education in the cabinet of each State Premier. In no one of the forty-eight American states is there anything approaching such a centralized system; the chief state officer even in those states where the state government is most active in educational matters is in no sense a director of education.[30] The American tradition of local responsibility is deeply rooted; each state is the sovereign power in regard to schools, but this power has been largely delegated to the school boards elected locally by the various cities, towns, and school districts.

There are at least two consequences of our highly decentralized system of public schools, one good, one bad. There is ample opportunity for experimentation and there is no lack of diversity, as anyone who tries to describe what is a typical high school soon discovers. Without this diversity and the healthy rivalry between cities and towns and between one state and another, our public secondary schools could hardly have succeeded as well as they have. The bad feature which visitors from other lands are quick to point out is the existence of some very inferior schools indeed. But on balance there can be no question but that the American people prefer the decentralized system with all its faults to a state system which might mean the elimination of some very poor schools but would also mean a high degree of uniformity within a given area. And this preference of the American electorate which is shared by public school administrators seems to be thoroughly sound. I have no doubt it will remain unchanged. The slowly increasing degree of fiscal support by the state has so far not been accompanied by a change of control of appointments or curricula. If local boards of education keep their vigor, the characteristically decentralized pattern of American schooling can be maintained.

In the face of the enormous diversity in secondary schools throughout the country, it is impossible to say what is the typical American scheme for educating adolescents. In some relatively well-to-do communities as many as 90 per cent of the youth aged 16 may be in school and over half may be planning to attend a college or university. In a highly industrialized section of a city only a relatively small percentage of those who start the last four years of a school course complete it and only a few per cent are likely to proceed with further education. Historically, in the older cities the pattern of secondary education was set in the nineteenth century by Latin Schools or Academies or High Schools which provided a classical curriculum of four to six years with two languages as an essential feature. As the number of students desiring to attend secondary schools increased, some school boards developed arrangements similar to those now characteristic of British education. Free schooling was provided for those who were able and willing to study subjects which forty years ago were considered essential as a preparation for college; those who did not attend these schools (roughly the equivalent of the present British Grammar Schools) were taken care of in other types of schools of a more technical and vocational nature. In other communities the high school was expanded in numbers and various alternative courses offered. One of these was often essentially a college preparatory course while others were largely devoted either to instruction in the use of tools or the development of skills used by bookkeepers and clerks in commercial undertakings.

For fifty years or more, educators have been heatedly discussing the curriculum of the ideal high school or the curricula of a group of high schools. The dual task of a secondary school — preparing for employment and preparing for further study — means that a variety of vocational pressures influences the curriculum. Where matters stand today in terms of statistics I do not pretend to know. I imagine that there are still many "old-fashioned" schools where reluctant youths are being exposed to a heavy dose of "book learning" unrelated to their interests and their ambitions. Nevertheless, in many cities and towns the pendulum has swung far in the opposite direction — so much so, that many friendly critics of public education believe that more emphasis should be placed on the type of instruction that is now given in those tax-supported schools of the British Commonwealth which are available for the gifted youth.

In every country the curriculum of a secondary school for the intellectually able students is connected with the demands of the faculties of the universities. The question of what is a "good" secondary education cannot be divorced from what the professors believe should be the knowledge and skills of the students that come to them from school. The differences between the British nations and the United States in regard to high school in no small measure reflect the vast differences in education for those 18 to 21 years of age. Therefore, before proceeding further with a discussion of the American high school and the plans for its future, it is necessary to examine the American college — its origin, its present status, and its future.

~ II ~

THE
AMERICAN COLLEGE

I T HAS OFTEN BEEN SAID that in the United States "everyone goes to college." This is far from the case, of course; less than a third of the potential students are enrolled either full time or part time in our colleges and universities. Nevertheless, as compared with the British nations, one might be tempted to make some such grossly exaggerated statement in order to emphasize the differences brought out by the estimates given in Table 4.[1] It would be just as fair to say in addition, "In England, Scotland, Australia, and New Zealand no one goes to college." For in the American sense of the word, no one does, for no such institution as the American college exists in any of the four countries. Oxford and Cambridge occupy today and have always occupied a special position. Their residential colleges provide a special kind of general education; in Oxford, in particular, certain combinations of studies (the Greats and the Modern Greats) offered a training that until recently at least was believed to be specially suitable for the future civil servant or politician. But aside from those two institutions, one can fairly say that the British universities are essentially professional schools,[2] and, one should add, professional schools with the highest standards.

In Great Britain and the nations of the British Commonwealth in general, a boy or girl enters a university at age 17 or 18 or 19 in order to obtain a professional education; the specialized course of study is over and done with for the

TABLE 4

Educational Patterns for University and College Students in Four British Countries and the United States 1950–1954 [1]

Percentage of Typical Age Group (Boys and Girls)
Attending Degree-granting Institutions Full Time

(Figures in parentheses are for full-time *and* part-time enrollments.)

Year in college or university (Class)	Eng-land	Scot-land	Australia [*]			New Zealand	U.S.A.[†]
			(1)	(2)	(3)		
1	3	4	3(6)	4.5(6)	6	3(5.5)	18(24)
2	3	4	3(6)	4.5(6)	6	3(5.5)	12(16)
3	3	4	3(6)	4.5(6)	6	3(5.0)	10(12)
4	<2	3		<2		<2	9(11)
5	<1	<1		<1		<1	1
6							1
7							<1

[*] (1) South Australia, (2) New South Wales, (3) Victoria.
[†] The figures in parentheses are those usually given because part-time and full-time students are listed together; but the best estimate is that one quarter of the total in the United States are part time.
Note: No allowance has been made for future military service or changing enrollments due to other causes, but the figures are not vitiated by any appreciable enrollment of World War II veterans. If the figures were for men only, they would be somewhat different: for England 4.5 instead of 3.0; Scotland 5.5 instead of 4; the Australian figures would be about 20 per cent larger as would be also those of the United States. The attempt to reduce the available data to a common basis involves assumptions that inflate somewhat the United States figures and make all the numbers significant only as to order of magnitude (see notes 1 and 3, pp. 111 and 114).

vast majority by the end of three or four years. In the United States, however, the elapsed time from the end of secondary school to a professional degree in law or medicine is five to eight years; even the bachelor's degree is with rare exceptions granted for not less than four years' study. Obviously it is not correct to say that in the United States a much larger percentage of our youth are attending a university than in

British nations; for such a statement implies that the meaning of the word "university" is the same in all English-speaking countries, which is far from being the case. This is brought out by the estimates given in Table 5 of the distribution of male students between general and professional courses.[3] A summary of the peculiarities of the picture in the United

TABLE 5

Estimated Enrollment of Male Students in
Colleges and Universities of the United States, 1950–1954
(Part Time and Full Time) *

Percentage of Typical Age Group Enrolled Full Time and Part Time

Year in College or University	Four-year College †	Profes- sional	Teacher Training	Junior College	Total
1	12	8	6	3	29
2	8	7	5	2	22
3	7	6	3	–	15
4	7	4	3	–	14
5	–	2	–	–	2
6	–	1	–	–	1
7	–	<1	–	–	<1

* These estimates are extremely tentative and uncertain and the method of presentation makes them somewhat too high in comparison with the figures for other nations. Some of the difficulties of preparing such estimates are explained in note 3 to this chapter.
† Including those majoring in business or commerce (nearly a third of the total in this column).

States might better be phrased in some such way as this: As contrasted to the British, Americans postpone specialization for several years (the study of engineering being an exception);[4] a relatively large percentage of American youth start towards professional study but the fraction finally emerging with a completed professional training is not much greater than in the nations of the British Commonwealth. In short, it is the existence of that special phenomenon the American college that both increases the numbers of students enrolled in the first few years of advanced education and postpones the completion of professional training.

Our system of selecting professional students as compared with the British is like a long giant funnel narrowing down gradually. The British system, a generation ago at least, was more like a long narrow cylinder. Even today the analogy between a funnel and a cylinder holds because throughout the British system there is far more attempt to select the pre-university students at an early age than here in the United States. But whether my mechanical analogy is appropriate or not, it is evident that the size of our secondary school enrollment as well as the length of our post-high school education is closely linked to the nature of American colleges. Indeed, I should be inclined to argue that a major factor in the United States in forcing the expansion of free secondary schools has been the four-year liberal arts college. The drive for general education for *all* American youth has been the consequence, I believe, of the great popular success of the nonprofessional college with its relatively slight emphasis on selection of those with intellectual talents.

Let me make it plain that I am firmly convinced that this increasing demand for general education has been well founded. The "degree of instruction" required for all American youth in this complex civilization can only be met by increased concern with a broad type of schooling.

When Thomas Jefferson wrote of his desire to cull "the natural aristocracy of talents and virtue," and educate it "at the public expense, for the care of the public concerns,"[5] he was expressing what has become a premise of all democratic nations: namely, that the taxpayer has a duty to supply the talented with the education necessary for the development of that talent. Why? Because such educated talent will later serve the taxpayer by serving the entire nation. In theory at least, the application of this doctrine could lead to confining secondary education to those who are especially gifted in terms of "book learning" and only to those so talented.

But even as great a democrat as Jefferson surely never had in mind denying opportunities for formal education to the adolescent sons of families who could afford to pay for whatever schooling they could find. At all events, neither on this continent nor anywhere in the British Empire in the nineteenth century did organized society attempt to make private secondary schools or colleges primarily schools for those of talent. Rather, the tendency was in the other direction. Private schools emphasized the importance of educating for life rather than preparing for a profession; religion was central to the educational process in many if not most Protestant church-connected schools as well as in the Catholic parochial schools. The life of the school and the importance of the playing fields, of the corporate spirit, and of loyalty were emphasized quite as much as the process of developing intellectual talent. So too by 1900 in the American college it was being said, "It isn't what you learn but the friends you make that matters."

By the mid-nineteenth century there were all sorts of private academies in the United States and an increasing number of privately endowed colleges. In Great Britain the old "Public Schools" were in process of revitalization, owing largely to the example of Arnold of Rugby. Their success enormously influenced the course of events in Australia, as I pointed out in the last chapter, and was not without its repercussions in the United States as well. For when, early in this century, the ideas of social democracy emerged throughout the English-speaking nations, the example of the popularity of the private school and college for those who could afford them became one driving force for using taxpayers' money for purposes less selective than Jefferson had in mind.

Whether or not the reader agrees with my diagnosis of the social and political forces that have operated in the last fifty years, there can be no doubt of the transformation (Table 6).[6] Forty years ago the pattern in this country was not far different from what it is today in the other English-speaking countries: the college enrollment was still only 5 per cent of the age group. By 1930, however, over 10 per cent of the 18- to 21-year-olds were enrolled in a degree-granting institution and by 1940 the percentage had risen to 15; the postwar figure after the tide of veterans has receded will probably be about 20 per cent.[7]

Clearly there has evolved on this continent an idea about the education of young men and women that is quite different from the ideas of the British in either Great Britain or the newer countries of Australia and New Zealand. The American college as a special type of institution has assumed a position of great importance. A "college education" has become accepted as a desirable experience and in this century degree-granting institutions have expanded in size enormously.

THE ORIGIN OF THE AMERICAN COLLEGE

To understand how the American concept of a liberal arts college arose, one must turn back the pages of history four hundred years, for all the educational patterns that I am comparing have a common origin, namely, late sixteenth-century England. A symbol of the basic cultural unity of the Anglo-Saxon world is the position of Shakespeare in the hierarchy of values implied in the teaching of literature in almost every school and college throughout the United States and the British Commonwealth. It is no accident that we all place the writings of an Elizabethan dramatist at the top of the list of what "every schoolboy should know."

England under Queen Elizabeth anglicized the Reformation; this English version of Calvinism provided the cultural basis for the seventeenth century; and it is in the seventeenth century that American educational history begins to diverge from the rest of the Anglo-Saxon pattern. Indeed, I am inclined to argue the paradoxical thesis that the late sixteenth- and early seventeenth-century English ideas about education have been perpetuated here on the North American continent, and it was the mother country, not the offspring, that departed from the original sixteenth-century tradition.

What I have in mind is simply this: In the first half of the

TABLE 6

The Change of the College Pattern in the United States

(All figures are for full-time attendance of both men and women.)

Year	Percentage of Youth 18–21 Attending College	Percentage of Age Group Graduating
1890	3	1.1
1900	4	1.8
1910	5	1.9
1920	8	2.7
1930	12	5.5
1940	15	7.9
1950	30 *	10.0 †

* Figure somewhat too high because of veteran enrollment; 20 per cent would be a more representative figure.

† Estimated for 1954 on basis of freshman enrollment for 1950.

seventeenth century, before the Civil Wars, Oxford and Cambridge were serving as educational centers for many young men who were not destined for the learned professions. The Reformation of the preceding century, while leaving the forms of education largely unchanged in these two ancient universities, had introduced the new spirit of the age. Theology, the admitted queen of the sciences in the Middle Ages, had become popularized. The same set of ideas that had opened the Bible to all also demanded that *all* should be able to read. The influence of John Knox's *Book of Discipline* on Scottish education I have already mentioned. Puritan and Presbyterian alike sought to provide free schools.

The history of Oxford and Cambridge from the Elizabethan settlement of the English Church to the outbreak of the Civil War in 1642 is the history of institutions seething with intellectual and political excitement. The opportunity to read and discuss the sacred writings bore fruit rapidly. The conflict between the High Church Party and the Puritans that finally led to a clash of arms had been going on for at least three generations in the colleges of Oxford and Cambridge before the Long Parliament was called. One of the demands of the Puritan party in that Parliament was that "the two fountains of learning" be cleansed, that is, purified from any leanings towards the Roman Church.[8]

Not only were the English universities in the early seventeenth century exciting places, but they were extraordinarily well attended. Something like a thousand young men entered Oxford and Cambridge each year in the first half of the seventeenth century. When one considers that the total population was about five million, this means in terms of the age group that perhaps as many as 2 per cent of the young men were in attendance in these two universities (there were, of course, no others).[9] After the Civil Wars the situation changed, and it is probably safe to say that not until the twentieth century did so high a proportion of the young men of England attend a university as in the first third of the seventeenth century.

The significant point is this. At the time to which I am directing attention, namely, the early decades of the seventeenth century, the role of the university was thought of not only in terms of training ministers, lawyers, doctors, but also in terms of educating gentlemen who were to take a leading part in public affairs. To document this statement would require a long digression. I shall content myself by noting: first, the very large attendance at the universities, in itself evidence that they were regarded as something other than theological and law schools; second, the large number of laymen who played historic parts in the struggle between King and Parliament who were former Oxford and Cambridge students; third, the significance of Puritan Oxford as a center of the new "experimental philosophy" during the Cromwellian period; [10] and fourth, the influence of Oxford and Cambridge men in the seventeenth-century settlements on the coast of North America.

As to the last point, some of the most striking evidence of the nature of Oxford and Cambridge education in the seventeenth century is provided by what was said by the founders of Harvard College. That a group of pioneers settling in a wilderness should have gone through with a scheme to start and operate a college within a generation of the settlement is a remarkable historical phenomenon. It is explicable only if one realizes how many Oxford and Cambridge men there were among the settlers. The English Puritan tradition was supersaturated with learning; it is not surprising, therefore, that when this tradition was transplanted to New England, the crystallization of a new university at once took place. To be sure, the Puritans required a learned ministry; it is easy to exaggerate, however, the significance of the famous phrase about the necessity of providing ministers when those among the immigrants should "lie in the dust." As Professor Morison has demonstrated, it was not a theological seminary but the replica of a Cambridge college that the New England settlers sought to establish in founding Harvard.[11] And through many ups and downs they and their descendants succeeded in keeping the college going, always with an eye on Oxford and Cambridge where so many of the founders had obtained their education.

Now we come to the divergence of the two streams — one American, the other British. The second half of the seventeenth century is to my mind the watershed between education in this country on the one hand and the educational tradition of all the rest of the English-speaking world on the other. Three significant events occurred in North America that have profoundly influenced all subsequent developments in the area that is now the United States. Oxford in 1648 and later Cambridge, both under Puritan control, recognized the Harvard A.B. as equivalent to their own degree; they admitted Harvard graduates to the Oxford and Cambridge A.M. without further examination.[12] Second, the College of William and Mary was chartered in 1693 and though the charter contains no explicit right to confer degrees, the implicit right must have been recognized in London, for degrees were awarded without question from the start. Third, in 1701 (I stretch the seventeenth century a bit) the Connecticut General Court chartered Yale and in so doing provided for the conferring of degrees.[13] Then in the middle of the eighteenth century three other institutions for the granting of degrees were chartered in North America: Princeton in 1746 by the Governor of New Jersey, Columbia (King's College) in 1754 by George II, and the University of Pennsylvania (College, Academy and Charitable School) in 1755 by "the proprietors and governor in chief of the Province of Pennsylvania."

Thus by the middle of the eighteenth century there were six colleges in the North American colonies granting at least the first degree in arts. Yet none of these institutions could be regarded as a true university because none had a faculty capable of examining for the higher degrees, at least by English and Continental standards. A precedent had been established that was to have a revolutionary effect on education. In the North American colonies the practice had become common for a college to grant the bachelor's degree to its graduates without reference to any other body of learned men. America had started down the road which in the twentieth century has led to the situation where American academic degrees are almost without meaning; the mere fact that an institution is a chartered college or university today in the United States is no guarantee of the quality of the instruction offered.

Six degree-granting colleges were established in North America by 1750, with apparently no protests from the mother country and no interest shown there in copying the new practice of the offspring. Probably what was happening across the Atlantic Ocean about such strictly academic matters as curricula and degrees excited no interest in London. The traditional guardians of the English degrees, Oxford and Cambridge, were enjoying what has been called "the corrupt sleep of the eighteenth century." If they had protested, the action of those same guardians in recognizing Harvard in 1648 might have been cited as a precedent against them. At all events, in the colonies, colleges granting degrees were established with no controls; at home Oxford and Cambridge continued unchallenged, except for the Scottish universities and Trinity College, Dublin, which had been chartered under Elizabeth.

THE BRITISH UNIVERSITY TRADITION

The monopoly of the two ancient seats of learning on the Isis and the Cam remained unbroken until the University of London was chartered in 1836. It not only remained unbroken but was narrowly confined by the Clarendon Code of the Restoration settlement (1661). Only those who subscribed to the doctrine of the Established Church were allowed to take degrees; with a few exceptions, only Church of England members were admitted even as students. As closed preserves neither Oxford nor Cambridge flourished. The dissenting academies that sprang up all over England in the mid-eighteenth century probably gave a much better education. It was in these academies rather than at Oxford and Cambridge that the seventeenth-century tradition of providing a gentleman's education was still vigorous. But of course these academies could not even think of granting degrees; they existed only by sufferance in a state formally committed to one Church only.

Thus it came about that when in the early nineteenth century there was renewed interest in expanding education in English-speaking communities, the United States and Great Britain proceeded in quite different ways. Nothing was more natural than that each one of the thirteen sovereign states of the new nation should express its sovereignty by reincorporating the college or colleges already existing within its territory and by chartering new colleges with the right to grant degrees. Between 1780 and 1836 no less than eighty colleges and universities were founded in the United States and empowered by the state legislatures to award the bachelor's degree to their graduates. Most of these were independent corporations, many of them church-affiliated, but some were state universities, a new type of institution in the English-speaking world. During this same period in Great Britain, one and only one new university was chartered, the University of London (whose significance for developments in Australia and New Zealand in the nineteenth century was equaled only by that of the Scottish universities). And it was Oxford and Cambridge that largely determined the nature of London University.[14]

The two ancient English universities had a consistent history of two centuries of fighting every effort to break their joint control of higher education. Even in the Cromwellian interlude this aspect of university life did not change, for we find a Puritan vice-chancellor of Oxford as vigorous in his opposition to establishing a new university at Durham as was his distant academic descendant in questioning the chartering of a university in London. When finally in 1836 after at least a decade of agitation, a degree-granting institution was established in the capital city of the British Empire, it was on the examining function of the university that stress was laid. University College, a completely secular college established in 1827, and King's College, a Church of England institution founded a few years later, became constituents of the new London University. Under the charter the University Senate, not the teaching bodies of either King's or University College, had the power to grant degrees based on adequate examination.[15]

An important principle was here either established or reaffirmed (depending on how one reads the history of the two preceding centuries); this principle was that the degrees to be conferred in England were to conform as far as possible to the high standards set by Oxford and Cambridge. The doctrine was laid down that the granting of the bachelor's degree was not to be separated from the right and ability to grant higher degrees. The dissimilarity here with the American picture is evident. Every new university in England and throughout the British Commonwealth in the nineteenth century was destined to be primarily a collection of professional faculties carefully guarding the high standards of the degrees conferred.

One must remember that for the first half of the nineteenth century Oxford and Cambridge were still closed preserves and "unreformed." From 1850 to 1870 the Royal Commissions of Inquiry and the ensuing Parliamentary legislation were slowly adapting the two ancient institutions to new conditions.[16] But it was not until the closing two decades of the nineteenth century that Oxford and Cambridge began to be considered by informed public opinion as leading modern universities. Relatively few of the graduates of the English "Public Schools" went on to these universities; thus the "Public Schools" were not essentially preparatory schools. Rather, to use a modern phrase, they "provided terminal education." To them was assigned the task of completing the education of those who would enter trade, industry, or public affairs. This idea of the role of the "Public Schools" was carried over to other parts of the British Empire in the second half of the nineteenth century, particularly to Australia.

EXPANSION OF AMERICAN COLLEGES IN THIS CENTURY

Here in the United States the course of history was quite different. As the nineteenth century wore on, degree-granting colleges more and more became the recognized media for maturing the leaders in all phases of public and commercial life. There was no restraining hand on experimentation with the curricula. Radical educational ideas could be introduced in the new Republic that were only discussed in England. Thomas Jefferson's proposals for the establishment of the University of Virginia is a case in point. The influence of what was projected in Virginia was felt in London. The Rockfish Gap Report of the Commissioners for the University of Virginia of 1818 was read and its revolutionary widening of the curriculum was eagerly welcomed by the London reformers.[17] But when actually established and given authority to grant degrees, London University was still largely a reflection of the orthodox pattern of sound learning.

The multiplicity of colleges in the United States and the absence of restraints favored new ideas but also failed to encourage the maintenance of high standards. In spite of some valiant efforts to provide advanced instruction and attract eminent scholars, the American college of the 1850's was in fact not very different in intellectual accomplishment from a British "Public School." And it served much the same purpose. But note well two important differences, the results of a long history. The American college granted an A.B. degree, and the course of study was usually four years. To be sure, this did not mean necessarily four years' longer exposure to formal education for the American college student as compared with his British equivalent who finished a "Public School." For the students entered American colleges at a younger age one hundred years ago than they do today. But the idea of a bachelor's degree as the hallmark of a four-year course following twelve years of school work became firmly fixed in the minds of the educated classes in the United States.

By the closing decade of the century it had become increasingly fashionable to go to college. The degree-granting institutions, now numbering several hundred, were not professional schools; rather they were colleges preparing their students for nonprofessional activities. Their curricula, the organization of student life, their pedagogic methods were the resultant of a hundred years of American experience. A new type of educational institution had become firmly established. The American college, whether or not it called itself a university, by 1890 was both catering to and generating an enormous popular demand for what was then called a liberal education and now is known as general education. This demand was soon to affect not only the expanding colleges but the secondary schools as well.

Three factors must be borne in mind in analyzing American schools and colleges as they existed at the close of the last century. One was the growing belief that a college had a good deal to offer besides formal study; sports, fraternities, extracurricular life in general were already looming large in the minds of the alumni who were celebrating their twenty-fifth year out of college when the nineteenth century disappeared. Another is the fact that many a poor boy had been able to attend an American college in the nineteenth century by borrowing a little money from a relative and working at odd jobs and during the summer. That a man had worked his way through college was nothing to be ashamed of in the United States in 1900; on the contrary, it was a matter of great pride. No similar way of financing an education has obtained in the British Empire with the possible exception of Scotland. Even in this century the relation of education to remunerative work in British nations is different from what prevails in America. [18]

The third factor directly influenced the American university rather than the American college, but had repercussions on the entire educational pattern. I refer to the Morrill Act of 1862 and the subsequent acts of Congress which made possible the land-grant colleges.[19] Here the Federal Government was the pacemaker in providing public monies for advanced education. The different states applied the subsidy for "agricultural and mechanical arts colleges" in different fashions. Some founded new colleges that shortly became rivals of the existing state university; others used the money to strengthen the state university. Whatever route was used, opportunities for a very wide range of practical higher education were increasingly afforded in the seventies, the eighties, and the nineties. All this had its influence on the movement for extending the privilege of free education to ever-expanding numbers. If a subsidized college was to be available to teach the mechanical arts and agriculture, free schools had to be ready to prepare boys and girls for these colleges. Particularly in the Middle West this extension of public education assumed increasing importance as the twentieth century came in sight.

I shall not underline the obvious difference between the United States with its high geographic mobility and rapidly-expanding social structure on the one hand and the stratified immobilized society of Great Britain on the other. Nor need I emphasize the egalitarian spirit so characteristic of the United States as early as the 1830's. Both were of importance in bringing about the expansion of American education. As to the doctrine of equality, I need only quote from De Tocqueville's *Democracy in America*. Speaking of the United States, he wrote:

"In that land the great experiment was to be made by civilized man, of the attempt to construct society upon a new basis; and it was there, for the first time that theories hitherto unknown, or deemed impracticable were to exhibit a spectacle for which the world had not been prepared by the history of the past." [20]

A few pages later he writes, "America, then, exhibits in her social state a most extraordinary phenomenon. Men are there seen on a greater equality in point of fortune and intellect, or in other words, more equal in their strength, than in any other country of the world, or in any age of which history has preserved the remembrance." [21]

And early in the same volume he declares, "The gradual development of the equality of conditions is therefore a providential fact, and it possesses all the characteristics of a Divine decree: it is universal, it is durable, it constantly eludes all human interference, and all events as well as all men contribute to its progress. . . None can say which way we are going, for all terms of comparison are wanting: the equality of conditions is more complete in the Christian countries of the present day than it has been at any time or in any part of the world; so that the extent of what already exists prevents us from foreseeing what may be yet to come." [22]

EXTENDING THE PRIVILEGES OF A COLLEGE EDUCATION

If you combine a belief in equality with a belief in the desirability of a full-time education leading to a collegiate degree for all who can afford it, the American pattern of education is the logical outcome. In simple form, the question may be thus stated: if a British "Public School" education or an American college education is a "good thing" even for those who are not going to do university professional work, why isn't it a good thing for everyone? This question has been asked explicitly or implicitly by an increasing number of people in the United States and also, in the last thirty years, in Great Britain and the British Commonwealth.[23] It should be noticed that these are quite different questions from the one to which Jefferson replied when he spoke of "culling the natural aristocracy of talents and virtue." He was answering the question: for whom is a special prolonged education to be provided at public expense? His answer is, only for those who are both talented and virtuous. But in increasing numbers the sons of the ruling class in Great Britain and the sons of the well-to-do in the United States were attending a "Public School" or a college whether or not they were talented and virtuous.

The English answer given in the Education Act of 1944 is essentially this: full time education at public expense up to and through the university should be provided for the intellectually talented, part-time vocational education for the rest after they finish school at age 16.[24] The British position is tenable only in a nation whose degree-granting institutions are highly selective and concerned chiefly with professional study. In the United States we have come perilously close to endorsing the view that a college education is a "good thing" for everyone; the only limitation has been expense, and working one's way through college has, for many, removed this hurdle. Having a multitude of colleges with no method of insuring any conformity to educational standards and emphasizing the nonintellectual side of college life, Americans could hardly claim that their colleges were selective. As to the lack of uniformity in regard to standards I may quote Henry Chauncey, President of the Educational Testing Service, who in reporting on the recent Selective Service tests has said, "A student who stands relatively low in one institution may compare very favorably, both in ability and in level of academic performance with a student who stands relatively high at another institution." [25]

College education in the United States, as the twentieth century moved on, came to be more and more justified as a preparation for citizenship. It was more and more divorced from any connection with professional training which was the province of a university: law, medicine, theology, and gradually the sciences with the exception of engineering came to be regarded as post-graduate subjects.[26] The logical outcome of all this development was a continuous demand for a wide variety of new subjects to be taught in school as well as college. The drive for general education — "education for citizenship" — affected the high schools even more than the colleges. At this point the expansion of the high schools began — and their transformation. In less than fifty years the pattern of full-time schooling, once similar to that now found in Australia, was completely altered.

THE RELATION OF SCHOOLS TO UNIVERSITIES IN BRITISH NATIONS

At this point I am going to ask the reader to take another look at education in the Antipodes, for I believe that the current practices in Australia and New Zealand and particularly the changes that have taken place throw consider-

able light on some of the problems that now confront us in
the United States.

As I pointed out earlier, tax-supported secondary schools
did not develop in Australia on any scale until the second
decade of this century. For those who could afford it, secondary education was provided by the private schools. In that
country, as throughout the British Empire fifty years ago, free
schools were provided for all children up to the age of ten or
eleven. Beyond this age, however, education was a highly
selective process except for those who could meet the costs
of a private school. The exceptional poor boy or girl could
win a scholarship at a private school and thus prepare for
the university. The first answer to the demand for greater
educational opportunity was to provide more scholarships or
"free places" in fee-charging schools (in England, the
ancient grammar schools often served this purpose). The
second answer, which was forthcoming sooner in Australia
than in the mother country, was to provide free secondary
schools giving a pre-university course of instruction but to
limit the enrollment by severe intellectual requirements.
The third answer was to provide, in addition to these
"academic" free schools, other types of schools for adolescents
who were intending to leave school at the age of fourteen or
fifteen. The fourth answer which has been given in New
Zealand and to a lesser degree in some Australian states, is
to experiment with a more comprehensive and less orthodox
type of secondary school curriculum. The views of the New
Zealand Minister of Education on the importance of such
experimentation I referred to in the preceding chapter.

The first step in modernizing (or some would say "Ameri-
canizing") the curriculum of the academic high schools in
New Zealand was to persuade the University of New Zealand
to alter its requirements for admission. For the curriculum
of the schools in New Zealand as in Australia has been until

recently closely controlled by a series of state examinations. Indeed, in all the Australian states and until a decade or so ago in New Zealand, the universities have held the whip hand over the schools both private and tax supported. Although only half of the graduates of the private schools attend the university, the curriculum of these schools is largely determined by the entrance requirements of the university in the state in which the school is located. (By and large, students do not cross state lines to attend a university in Australia and until a few years ago there was only one university in each state.) Furthermore, examinations set by the Ministry of Education in each state (external examinations) are required at various steps in the educational journey even for those who are pursuing a nonacademic course.[27]

Indeed, I have ventured the opinion to some of my Australian acquaintances that their education was examination-ridden and certificate-bedeviled, to which I received the reply that this was in the British tradition. Since the days when Macaulay started the competitive examinations for the Indian Civil Service and London University was established as an examining body, certified educational experience has been demanded.[28] In Australia employers demand a "leaving certificate" from the schools. This certificate or its equivalent is granted only on the basis of success in an external examination — that is, an examination set by a state board on which university people are well represented.

The private schools, Catholic and Protestant alike, and the tax-supported schools are all affected by the system of external examinations. (In South Australia there are four such examinations at ages 14, 15, 16, and 17 respectively, the last taken only by those who proceed to the university.) From the point of view of the university there is much to be said for a rigid secondary school curriculum of English, one or two foreign languages, algebra, geometry, physics, and chemistry. If a university is regarded primarily as a group of professional faculties with high standards, it might seem logical to insist that all entrants have the same pre-professional education. And the conditions in Australia have been peculiarly advantageous for enforcing such an arrangement since in each state the tax-supported schools are knit into a tight system operated by the Ministry of Education.[29]

This system, at first sight ideal from the professors' point of view, is in process of breaking down, or some would say, being modernized. What happened in New Zealand is the extreme example. A "common core" of studies was introduced, the emphasis on languages reduced, the study of science made less a formal mastering of "first year" chemistry and physics. The effect on the power of the school to hold students until graduation was as expected. But to bring about these changes the University of New Zealand had to be persuaded to turn over to the schools the selection of those who were permitted to proceed to the university. The power of the external examiners was practically abolished.[30]

Changes in the examinations and curriculum have taken place in New South Wales, but they are not as drastic as in New Zealand; the relations between the university and the schools have not been basically altered. As the curriculum was broadened, the list of subjects on which future university students could be examined was lengthened. This was inevitable, for if room is to be provided in the school curriculum for such modern subjects as history, geography, social studies, music, art, and needlework for girls, there must be some inducement in terms of examinations. At all events, the professors in the university can no longer count on *all* their students having essentially the same preparation. But by American standards they are all "well prepared"; even after the modernizing of the curricula in New South Wales about a quarter of all the students in school age 15–16 were studying two foreign languages and another 10 or 12 per cent, one foreign language.[31]

Chancellor McConnell of Buffalo in his account of general education in England, commenting on the extreme specialization in the universities, states: "And in England . . . this professionalism extends downward into the grammar school." [32] But he asks how this fact can be reconciled with the widespread opinion that the English university graduates are "people of wide knowledge and cultivation." The explanation of the paradox he finds to reside largely in the family background of those who have hitherto formed the majority of university students. My own observations agree completely with his diagnosis, but I should emphasize a little more the significance of the residential aspects of Cambridge and Oxford. For what these colleges accomplished in the nineteenth century and the first quarter of the twentieth century for one class of student has set a standard for the cultivated gentleman. But whether such informal and highly expensive methods can continue to operate in the future I have doubts, as have some English educators. To find a less expensive substitute for the general education provided by a "collegiate way of life" is the aim of the American senior high school and many a college. Indeed, on this point I may venture to quote from myself:

Faith in the value of general education . . . is now fairly widespread among college teachers in the United States (though as to methods of attaining the objective there is widespread disagreement). Yet it is well to remember that only on the continent of North America is it believed by English-speaking peoples that some formal educational exposure to the natural sciences beyond the age of eighteen is desirable for the future man of affairs or lawyer or social scientist or humanist. And correspondingly, outside of the United States and Canada it is rare for the future scientist, engineer, or doctor to undertake after the age of seventeen any formal study of the social sciences or the humanities.[33]

By experimenting with various types of college courses, we in the United States are attempting to find the modern equivalent of the kind of liberal education that was once the product of "the collegiate way of life" — the ideal of the founders of the first colleges in colonial days. When literacy could be defined only in terms of languages, literature, and history, the task of a college was relatively easy. An "education around the dinner table" was, even in the nineteenth century, education within a relatively narrow field of knowledge. Furthermore, those who came to the universities then were already, for the most part, from highly literate families. In England even a generation ago, the well-endowed residential colleges of Oxford and Cambridge could enroll a majority of students from homes well stocked with books. Today, however, I doubt whether anywhere in the world the mere device of collegiate living (excellent though such a way of life may still be for young men with intellectual ambitions) suffices to provide the beginnings of a general education. The cultural background of the students is too diverse, the impact of modern science and scholarship has been far too great. These two factors have made necessary a reëxamination of the older idea of a liberal education.

General education cannot be dissociated from the family background of the students. Furthermore, it cannot be wholly dissociated from vocational ambitions. To reconcile this fact with the desire to keep our youth as undifferentiated as possible at the high school age is one of the many really difficult problems facing the American high school. I shall have more to say on this subject in the next chapter. The same problem arises in our colleges.

A ruthless critic might claim that much of what is offered to the American college student as general education is only highly vocational training dressed up in fancy academic language. To some degree such criticisms have validity.

How far the development of special skills is a proper function of a university is an open question. Certainly few would care to defend such absurdities as courses in "fly casting" which count towards a degree. Our whole system of intercollegiate athletics with the emphasis on gate receipts and the recruitment of players is likewise open to ridicule by observers from other nations. The truth of the matter seems to be that in the vast chaotic mass of so-called "higher education" in the United States one can find almost anything one wishes either to praise or to condemn. As regards the numbers and diversity of institutions there is nothing faintly resembling it anywhere in the world. There are still many talented boys and girls who drop out of education far too soon; there are many less able who continue far too long. Yet on the whole, the American people applaud the American college and urge forward the drive for general education. The goal for many educators is full-time schooling for everyone to at least 18 and some college education for as many as 50 per cent of those 19 and 20.[34]

The assumption that a general education on a full-time basis is a "good thing" for every youth who can afford it, when combined with the doctrine of "equality of opportunity," would appear to leave no logical alternative to a much further expansion of college education than has yet taken place even in the United States. Yet almost everyone is vaguely aware of certain difficulties in this argument. Are we sure that full-time education up to age 21 or 22 is beneficial for all types of individuals? Perhaps colleges after all were supposed to be concerned with developing intellectual talent; perhaps there should be some selection of the more rather than the less talented even among those who can afford to pay their way. Possibly, attempts to give a general education to the average good all-around boy at the college level interferes to some extent with the training of the "natural aristocracy of talents and virtue" to which Jefferson referred. It can even be argued by those who hold strongly to the egalitarian premise that less than four years of college together with part-time employment might provide the best education for many sons of the rich if it suffices for many children of the poor. What is needed, perhaps, is not an expansion of four-year college and university enrollment but a reëvaluation of what is the ideal education for different sorts of boys and girls irrespective of their family income. Possibly a four-year college education is no longer the privilege that those of us who are urging students to attend our institutions have so long assumed.

In the next chapter I shall venture to give one man's answers to the questions suggested by these doubts.

⁓ III ⁓

LOOKING AHEAD

IN THE LAST TWO CHAPTERS I endeavored to range rather widely in both time and space in order to examine the origin and present functioning of secondary schools in a modern democracy. I asked the reader to consider varied developments of a common tradition that had its origin in Great Britain nearly four centuries ago. In particular I directed attention to the various present answers to the two-fold problem presented by Thomas Jefferson: namely, first, how can a nation best cull "the natural aristocracy of talents and virtue" and prepare it "by education at the public expense for the care of the public concerns"; and second, what "degree of instruction" is today required in order that our liberties may be safe "in the hands of the people."

One feature common to all the countries examined is the considerable expansion of tax-supported education of adolescents in the last forty or fifty years. In large part this can be accounted for, I believe, by the success of the English "Public School" (or its equivalent) on the one hand and the American liberal arts college on the other, coupled with a growing belief in the doctrine of equality of opportunity. If a long general education appears to be a necessity for those who can pay for it, public opinion tends increasingly to insist that it likewise be considered a necessity for those who have been less fortunate in the financial status of their parents.

In this chapter I propose to make certain suggestions about the future development of American schools and colleges. Before doing so, perhaps I should give in a few words my own educational credo in order to lay bare my prejudices, for try as one may to be impartial, no educator can be an unbiased reporter or historian in the field of education.

According to my view, the doctrine of equality of which De Tocqueville wrote so long ago has come to mean in the United States not parity of status for all adults but equality of opportunity for the young. This ideal implies, on the one hand, a relatively fluid social structure changing from generation to generation, and, on the other, mutual respect between different groups; in short, a minimum of class distinction. The vast expansion of secondary education in the United States in this century has created a new means for forwarding the American concept of democracy. If we so desire, we can, through our schools, annually restore a great degree of fluidity to our social and economic life and in so doing make available for the national welfare reservoirs of potential professional talent now untapped. At the same time, by stressing the democratic elements in our school life and in the organization of our schools, we can promote the social and political ideals necessary for the harmonious operation of an economic system based on private ownership and the profit motive, but committed to the ideals of social justice. The nearer we approach, through the management of our schools, to our goal of equality of opportunity (which, however, admittedly never can be reached), and the better we teach the basic tenets of American democracy, the more chance there is for personal liberty to continue in the United States.

PROGRAM FOR THE FUTURE

Such are the biases with which I approach the question of the future of the secondary schools and colleges in the United

States. Within a few years the number of adolescents in this country will be 50 per cent greater than at present. Looking forward to that time, I suggest that:

(1) We do not expand our four-year colleges either as to number or as to size.

(2) We do not expand the four-year programs in our universities; rather, we contract them.

(3) We attempt to make a two-year college course (following the regular high school course) fashionable; to this end we might award a bachelor's degree of general studies to the graduates of such colleges.

(4) We endeavor to create a climate of opinion in which the length of the education beyond eighteen is *not* considered the hallmark of its respectability.

(5) We continue the expansion of our junior and senior high schools to meet the new bulge in the enrollments, but in so doing, recognize the need for remaking the curriculum in many schools.

(6) We adhere to the principle of a comprehensive high school with a common core of studies and differentiated special programs, but in so doing we make far more effort to identify the gifted youth and give him or her more rigorous academic training in languages and mathematics.

(7) We explore the success of some high schools in recent years with "work experience programs" and expand these programs, including particularly the thirteenth and fourteenth grades (the two-year college).

(8) We provide by private and public action for more scholarships for high school graduates, but only for those who are potential professional men and women (advanced education for others should in general be offered locally by two-year terminal colleges).

(9) We endeavor to transform all the present four-year colleges into institutions with high academic standards and

arrange the curricula with the thought that a majority of students in these colleges will go on to professional training after two, three, or four years, depending on the ability and drive of the individual.

(10) We continue to experiment with general education at every level for the future manual worker, the future salesman or executive, and the most highly specialized university graduate.

Coupled with these ten suggestions I venture to address one to the faculty members of the universities and colleges which now maintain high standards: Stop wringing your hands and complaining about the poor preparation of the students from secondary schools; rather, lend a hand to those in charge of these schools and those teaching in them and in so doing learn something about their problems. Furthermore, consider the advisability of returning to the practice of forty years ago by offering some inducement to the bright boy or girl in high school to study languages, science, and mathematics; for example, let proficiency in these subjects shorten the college course or lighten the load of academic work in a four-year program.

These proposals contemplate an eventual shift in the educational pattern of the United States. The percentage of an age group attending secondary schools at age 14 to 18 would be, if anything, increased; so too would the percentage of the 18 to 20 year olds attending a local two-year college. But the percentage of the total number 18 to 22 years old enrolled in four-year liberal arts colleges and four-year university programs would be decreased by at least a half. Note, I propose to accomplish this not by cutting back the present size or number of four-year colleges but simply by failing to expand them when the "wave of the future" — the increased numbers of youth — shall reach their doors.[1]

There is little that is novel in these suggestions. They imply a continuation of that drive for general education which is so characteristic of the United States. They reflect a belief in the value for *all* American youth of a study of history, the elements of political science, economics, sociology, and geography, some illustrations of the methods of the natural sciences, together with a study of literature and the arts conducted with due regard for developing emotional maturity and wisdom. This belief — a naive faith, a British educator has called it — in general education is to be contrasted with the belief in the other English-speaking lands in the value of the prolonged study of one or two foreign languages, mathematics through geometry, and an orthodox first year course in physics and chemistry.[2]

My proposals are also based on my conviction that as far as possible the public schools in the United States should be schools where the youth of very different backgrounds and outlooks share a common experience, where the extracurricular activities and at least a common core of studies including English should cut across vocational interests and cover a wide range of scholastic aptitudes.[3] In planning the curricula of such schools we might move still further in the direction of flexibility as between different types of high school programs even if this means postponing until 17 or even 19 the decision of who is to be a university student. The collegiate education of those who have little aptitude for book learning, I believe, might be shortened by two years and the professional training and collegiate education of the others somewhat compressed. In short, if we could make those who pay for it less inclined to waste time and money on prolonging their education unduly, we might be more effective in spending public funds for schools and colleges.

British observers are critical of American education on many grounds. But the most pertinent criticism, to my mind, is that expressed by some such phrase as "What a luxurious system, how wasteful of time and money; only a very rich nation could afford it." I am inclined to question how much economics has been a determining factor in the past history of British education, although financial considerations undoubtedly put limits on the plans for expansion in Great Britain now. Religion, class feeling, political ideals, and public opinion on cultural matters (fashion, if you will) have been at least as effective agents as the supply of dollars or pounds sterling. Yet I believe for many students the courses of study in the schools and colleges of the United States today are unnecessarily wasteful of time, at least; our education needs tightening up, as it were, and my suggestions are directed to that end.[4]

THE COMPREHENSIVE HIGH SCHOOL

The American concept of secondary education is differentiated from the British not only because of our commitment to education for *all* but because of the development of the comprehensive high school. Those concerned with public education have increasingly become advocates of one school that serves all the youth of a community. Within this one school there can be and must be differentiation of courses of study, but ideally there should be some part of the formal program shared by all the students. The unity of the school, however, like that of a British "Public School" comes from regarding the institution as a social unit. The extracurricular activities provide the media through which students from widely different walks of life come to know one another. Almost all the arguments in favor of a British "Public School" (or its Australian counterpart) as a training ground for citizens can be given in favor of a comprehensive high school.

The type of secondary school I have been discussing has been described in a publication by the Educational Policies

Commission of the National Education Association.[5] It takes somewhat different forms, depending on whether the community to be served is an urban or a rural area. The description is admittedly a blueprint of an ideal, but close approximations to it can be found in many towns and small cities in the United States. I am convinced that progress lies in the direction of improving such schools and transforming other types of secondary education to conform with such models. Before discussing the scholastic program of such a school, let me discuss briefly the pros and cons of this arrangement for secondary education.

Without attempting a scholarly investigation of the subject, I hazard the opinion that the idea of a comprehensive high school is a product of the special history of this nation. Certainly there was nothing in the English tradition which favored this idea. In England we find Grammar Schools with a five- or six-year curriculum for those of high scholastic aptitude who cannot afford to attend the "Public Schools." For the education of other adolescents other types of secondary schools are only now being developed.[6] The English tradition was also characteristic of the urban areas of the northeastern part of the United States at the close of the nineteenth century. In Boston, for example, even fifty years ago, the public school system included a Latin School (which can claim a continuous history of more than three centuries) with a six-year course of study, an English High School (characterized by the absence of Latin from an otherwise fairly orthodox four-year curriculum), and a Mechanics Art High School. Certain of the nearby suburban areas, however, were served by local high schools which were in part college preparatory schools and in part schools for those who were not going to college.

Today in the larger cities of the United States the separation of students into different schools depending on their academic ability and their vocational ambitions is common practice. I have become increasingly convinced that such an arrangement is a mistake, for it fails to provide a basis for the growth of mutual understanding between different cultural, religious, and occupational groups. The primary public schools by and large do provide this opportunity; so too do the high schools in the towns and small cities. Indeed, without this unifying influence of the public school, I doubt if the American nation could have developed its remarkable coherence in spite of its great size and cultural diversity. The task of assimilating many strains of migrations has been accomplished but the job of nourishing the spirit of democratic unity continues. If the battle of Waterloo was won on the playing fields of Eton, it may well be that the ideological struggle with Communism in the next fifty years will be won on the playing fields of the public high schools of the United States. That this may be so is the fervent hope of all of us who are working to support and improve these characteristic American institutions.

The concept of education as a social process, combined with a belief in the American idea of democracy and a concern with national unity, lead to the conclusion that a first-rate comprehensive high school is the ideal. But one must freely admit that there are many cities and towns where such schools do not exist or where they fall far short of the ideal. Leaving aside the special problem of segregation in the southern states, one must recognize the existence of social forces that tend to nullify the cohesive character of the high school. For example, in a city or town too large to be served by one high school, the concept of an undifferentiated school leads to the establishment of several high schools, each serving a given area. Yet in a neighborhood that is too heavily polarized by group cleavages, the high school has difficulty in operating as an effective social unit. A section of a city that includes both very low-rent tenements and costly apartment houses will not have a comprehensive high school that includes all the youth of the area. The children of the upper income families will be sent to schools elsewhere. As conditions stand today in some cities and towns, the principal of a high school whose students are required to come from a certain sector is going to have a difficult if not impossible job to provide a meeting ground for disparate types of students. But the existence of these problems does not spell the failure of the comprehensive high school; it only points to the need for planning educational development with an eye to sociology as well as pedagogy.[7]

Some cities or towns once sufficiently homogeneous to have been happily served by a high school have become converted into communities where antagonistic cultural groups destroy most of the advantages of a comprehensive school. Parents who live in such communities, and who can afford it, have three choices: They can move to another section of the metropolitan area where a comprehensive high school is operating successfully; they may send their children to private schools; they may put up with the high school at hand in spite of the social difficulties. Of these courses, the first would seem to me far and away the wisest. For those youth today are really fortunate who can attend a local public secondary school where boys and girls with a variety of religious and economic backgrounds study and play together. The majority of young Americans are now enjoying these advantages. That this is so is the principal reason that I for one have confidence in the future of this nation.

EDUCATION OF THE GIFTED

As I have sometimes been accused of painting an idealized picture of American public schools, let me here consider briefly some of their shortcomings. To my mind, first and foremost among these is their failure to be sufficiently concerned with the intellectually able youth. There is no reason why within a comprehensive high school well supported by the community a boy or girl who has academic ability cannot receive a good education. But the number of such schools in which those of high intellectual ability receive adequate stimulus and sound instruction is far too few. There is a false antithesis in the minds of too many people (including some educators) between education for *all* American youth and education for the gifted. For the American public high school to continue to fulfill its purpose, any idea of an opposition between these two functions of secondary schools must be eliminated.[8]

My continuing plea to public high school superintendents, principals, and teachers is that they must be far more effective in identifying the academically able youth and be more concerned with preparing him for university education. One meets a spirit of defeatism in this regard among high school people in some cities. They sometimes feel that the able youngsters of the families who can afford it are bound to be taken out of their schools largely for social reasons and that there is no use competing with private college preparatory schools. This attitude is reinforced by the existence within the city system of certain schools that prepare for college while others are strictly vocational.

There is a great deal of mythology in this whole business of the relation of school to college. The records of high school boys in Eastern colleges heavily patronized by the sons of the well-to-do who attended private schools show that the public school graduate more than holds his own in the competition.[9] I could name high schools said to be incapable of preparing boys for college whose graduates time and again do remarkably well in colleges and universities with high standards. But all this does not mean that there are no high schools so inferior from the point of view of both curricula and pedagogy as to make it very difficult for one of their graduates to undertake a stiff college course. Nor does it mean there is not much time wasted in high school by the future professional man or woman — time which should be used in acquiring such skills as advanced mathematics and the reading and writing of French or German.[10]

The lack of uniformity in our secondary schools (a product of our freedom and diversity) makes it difficult to generalize. Therefore, while urging many high schools to place more emphasis on the thorough study of conventional subjects, I must at the same time urge other schools to broaden their curricula. Fifty years ago the public high school in most localities was largely a college preparatory school, the prestige of a classical course was very great, and an orthodox academic course was presented. To fit *all* American youth into such narrow scholastic bounds was an impossibility. It was recognized a generation ago by alert educators that if we were to provide full-time education until the age of 17 or 18 for two-thirds or three-quarters of our adolescents, a varied and wide curriculum must be arranged. This idea, however, has still not been accepted by some Boards of Education. In these cases the need is not for emphasis on the gifted so much as for concern with general education.

I do not propose to discuss in any detail the organization of secondary education. The old separation between "grammar school" (ending at the eighth grade) and the four-year high school has now given way quite generally to another arrangement in which the junior high school plays an important part.[11] But in general the tendency has been to postpone the differentiation in curricula until the ninth and tenth grades (ages 14 to 15). Indeed, since many of our colleges and universities have very flexible entrance requirements and almost no standards for degrees, it becomes possible for an able boy or girl to shift as late as 18, 19 or 20 from a strictly vocational curriculum to a college and eventually to professional university work. This is one great advantage that comes from the chaotic arrangement of colleges with a wide range of standards. Every now and then a young man of great ability, imagination, and drive enters a profession by a highly circuitous route.

Whether a high school student is to enter a two-year college, a four-year college, an engineering school, or take a job on graduation is a highly important decision. There are great advantages in postponing it until as late as possible. Family status is much less likely to influence such a decision at age 17 than at age 11+. Therefore, those who favor a high social mobility will favor undifferentiated secondary education to as late an age as possible. Forcing an early decision about "going to college" works against the recruitment of talent for the professions and thus against the welfare of our industrialized society. Finally, while a decision in terms of intellectual ability can possibly be made as well at 11+ as at 15+, in terms of other factors it cannot.

In the first chapter I noted the current difficulties in England arising from the necessity of selecting boys for free Grammar School places as early as 11. For some families with professional traditions and without sufficient funds to pay for a "Public School" education, the existence today of relatively few places in local grammar schools, which have become highly selective, is a hardship. In Australia the existence in each city of relatively inexpensive private schools preparing for the university provides an escape mechanism from such a predicament.

If one can speak of a typical American arrangement when such wide variety exists, it would be fair to say that in the United States we attempt little differentiation in our public schools until age 15. As a consequence, the American student enrolled in a public school studies few of the academic subjects believed essential for university work in Great Britain or Australia. Furthermore, he rarely studies any of them as intensely as the corresponding boy or girl in the other English-speaking countries.

We can correct this situation somewhat and to good advantage within the framework of a comprehensive high school. But we cannot correct the situation to the degree that those accustomed to the British or Continental tradition would think wise. For these foreign observers have not thought through the contrast between a selective system of education starting at 11 or 12 and a system of general secondary education. There are advantages in the British system to the individual in terms of the mastery of intellectual skills, but they are far outweighed, to my mind, by the negative factors. Under our system, which in the last chapter I likened to a wide funnel as contrasted with the British narrow cylinder, our students make their decision to enter a university at a relatively mature age.

To illustrate the complexities of the relation between school, college, and university, let me insert a few words about one recurrent problem. It is generally assumed that the United States needs a continuing supply of physicists, chemists, and engineers in large numbers. Yet the number of students failing in scientific courses in colleges, universities, and engineering schools each year is high, the attrition is heavy. Among the reasons that have been suggested is the failure of the high schools to prepare their students adequately in physics, chemistry, and mathematics. Too many times, it is said, the student not only has studied little algebra in school but has come to hate it! This is one of the many charges and countercharges that are made so easily and documented with so much difficulty. There are always many hidden assumptions in educational arguments of this sort.

For example, the adequacy or inadequacy of a high school course as preparation for a definite college program clearly depends on what the college teacher expects of his students. If, for example, those in charge of a first year course in physics in an engineering school assume that the freshman should enter with a knowledge of trigonometry, then many high schools in the United States are preparing their students inadequately. This example I give only to illustrate the point that college specialization can strike its roots deep into the secondary school course.

In the British pattern this interrelation of the specialization in a university and in a school is taken for granted. In one Australian university the professor of chemistry was quite definite that unless a student entered the university with a solid high school course in physics and chemistry, he could not study chemistry. (And by a "solid high school course" a Britisher will mean the equivalent of a freshman college course in the U.S.A.) I mention this case to emphasize the early age at which in British countries specialization for those who are to be scientists must begin. Now in the United States, where our feelings in general are adverse to such early commitment to one academic road, the college teachers are by no means of one mind as to how much previous exposure to their subject they advise. A few college professors of chemistry, for example, would prefer students who had never studied chemistry in high school, but who were well trained in physics and mathematics. Yet the study of chemistry, physics, and biology is more and more being distributed throughout the high school years. The intrusion of general science even into the elementary schools presents special problems to secondary school teachers. The whole subject of the relation of school specialization in science and mathematics to the training of scientists and engineers needs further exploration in this country. I have no final answers to the many problems which stud the interface between high school and college, but I am sure these problems are worthy of far more impartial investigation than they have as yet received.

EQUALITY OF OPPORTUNITY

To me, it is interesting to compare the various blocks that stand in the way of a university education for a poor but talented boy in the countries I have been considering in this book; or, to put the matter in other language, what factors in each country limit the application of the doctrine of equality of opportunity. Here in the United States there can be no question that the limitation is often financial. We are losing a vast amount of talent particularly in small cities, towns, and in the country because the boy from a poor family cannot afford to go to a college or university which can develop his potentialities. Measures should be taken to remedy this situation; to this proposal among my ten I would give high priority. We are likewise losing talent because in some communities many able students are not interested in going to college. The improvement of educational guidance in the high schools should result in an increase in the percentage of the very able who proceed with their education.

A quick survey of the other countries considered indicates that in Australia and probably in New Zealand the financial hurdle has been largely eliminated. Yet the reader will recall that relatively few students, by American standards, go on with full-time education after high school. The new Commonwealth Scholarship Scheme in Australia is in a sense a continuation of their G.I. Bill.[12] It involves the expenditure of the equivalent, in terms of the national income, of several hundred million dollars in the United States for university scholarships; the impact of this scheme is just beginning, the enrollment of the universities is expected to rise. In the future, at least, the blocks to finding the best of the potential talent for professional training will be in Australia related to social and educational considerations rather than financial.

The attractive force of degree-granting institutions may be too great in the United States; but it is far too feeble in Australia. What the well-to-do and the future industrial manager feel unnecessary, the poor boy is not likely to desire; hence the loss in enrollment in the later years of the tax-supported schools to which I referred in a previous chapter. (Efforts are being made in Australia to meet the economic drawing power of a job by granting subsidies for living expenses of students in school, even for boys and girls living at home. But one may be skeptical as to the success of attempts to have scholarships compete financially with jobs.) The advantage of having so many young people in the United States attend colleges of even low academic standing is that among the many who come to enjoy, a few remain to work. And from this group come some very able professional people. The mere fact that full-time education until 18 is now the rule rather than the exception sets the fashion. There are still many sociological, rather than economic, factors which keep boys and girls with high I.Q.'s from going to college; but these factors, I feel sure, operate to a far lesser degree in the United States than in any other nation.

WORK EXPERIENCE PROGRAMS AND PART-TIME EDUCATION

There are many youths who, irrespective of the family fortune, would like to earn money, to have a job, even as young as 15. The advantages of work experience for high school students have been increasingly emphasized in recent years. High school administrators and teachers are no longer saying to employers, "We want our boys and girls back in our classrooms." Rather, they are saying, "Work experience is a valuable part of a young person's education. We want you to continue to employ some of our students for some of their time. We will continue to teach them in school and share in their supervision so that they can learn as much as possible from their experience in working with you, and we will give them credit for this work if it is done satisfactorily to you and to us."

A survey in 1947 indicated that about 50 per cent of the high schools in cities of twenty-five thousand or more had some kind of work experience program for their pupils. A study made in the spring of 1950 of thirty-eight cities in eighteen states showed that in nearly all high schools some credit toward graduation was granted for work experience though in no city did the proportion of high school students in the work experience program exceed 10 per cent of the total enrollment.[18] One must remember that to a considerable degree this development is a postwar phenomenon. Furthermore, it is by no means easy to work out arrangements with local employers and the local unions for such programs. But the trend is in the right direction; if employment stays high, there can be and should be, to my mind, a far larger number of students in these programs. This should be particularly so in the two-year colleges (thirteenth and fourteenth grades) which I suggest should be substituted for an expansion of our four-year colleges.

A group of educators drawing a blueprint of the future have laid down the following set of principles to govern the work experience programs:

1. The pupil must be regularly enrolled in the school so that the school can control his work experience. Credit is given only if there is evidence that useful learning has occurred.

2. The work experience must be related to the pupil's total educational program, either vocational or cultural. However, if a student has not yet developed specialized cultural or vocational aims, learning to work well at almost any job may properly be considered part of his education.

3. To insure continued learning, work experience must be supervised by a member of the professional staff of the school.

4. Work experience must be so organized as to produce continuous growth in skills and knowledge. Repetitive work should not be continued long after all available learning value has been extracted from it. On the other hand, learning to work industriously, to report for work on time, and to continue one job beyond the limits of pleasure and novelty are valuable achievements.[14]

It is interesting to contrast what is developing here in the United States with the British answers to the same and related problems. In Great Britain, Australia, and New Zealand the idea of working one's way through school and college has never been accepted as it has here in America. Conditions are now altering somewhat, but, by American standards, part-time work done while a student is still in school or college is a relatively rare phenomenon. Rather, the situation is just reversed, at least in some Australian states. In these states, particularly in the cities, there is a vast amount of part-time education for youth from fourteen to twenty-two. I understand a similar pattern is projected for England. I have heard it stated that the goal of the new English system is full-time education for everyone to age 16 and compulsory part-time education for everyone to age 18, except for about 15 per cent of each age group who will receive full-time schooling to 18. The 1951 pattern for males is shown by the figures in Table 7; the high percentage of those enrolled part time in age groups 15–19 is very striking.[15]

TABLE 7

English Educational Pattern (1951)

Distribution of Boys and Young Men between Schools and Other Educational Institutions on a Full-Time and Part-Time Basis in England and Wales

(assuming no military service before completion of course)

Percentage of Age Group (Male) Enrolled

Age Group	Full Time (Schools)				Full Time (Other Institutions)				Part-Time Education		
	Publicly Maintained	Publicly Aided	Independent Recognized	Other	Further Education Establishments	Teacher Training Colleges	Universities	Total Full Time	Day	Evening	Total *
14	88.5	2.5	4.5	3.5	—	—	—	99.0	—	—	—
15	23.0	2.0	4.0	2.0	1.0	—	—	32.0	11.0	35	40
16	9.0	1.5	3.0	1.5	1.0	—	—	16.0	15.0	38	45
17	4.0	0.5	2.0	1.0	1.0	—	—	8.5	14.0	36	43
18	2.0	0.5	0.5	0.5	1.0	1.0	2.0	7.5	9.0	22	26
19	—	—	—	—	1.0	1.0	4.5	6.5	5.5	18	22
20	—	—	—	—	1.0	—	4.5	5.5	4.0	11	13
21	—	—	—	—	1.0	—	4.0	5.0	3.0	9	10
22	—	—	—	—	0.5	—	2.5	3.0	2.5	9	10
23	—	—	—	—	0.5	—	1.0	1.5	2.0	9	10

* The total is less than the sum of those attending day and evening classes, as there is some duplication. It will be noted that the total enrolled full time *and* part time is 72 per cent for age group 15, 61 per cent for age 16, and 52 per cent for age group 17. For the United States the same age groups have 88, 76, and 61 per cent enrolled full time (Table 1, Chapter I, p. 3). For the older groups the U.S. figures are for boys and girls in school *or* college (1940 Census returns): 18 years, 36 per cent; 19 years, 20 per cent; 20 years, 12 per cent. There are no adequate data for part-time enrollments in the United States. (See Chapter II, note 1, page 111.)

To analyze further the working of a part-time system, some statistics from Australia (Tables 8 and 9) are of interest.

For many purposes it is desirable to see the educational pattern for boys apart from girls. This is particularly true in regard to part-time vocational training and professional education. For Sydney (metropolitan area, population about

TABLE 8

Estimated Distribution of Boys and Girls in Schools, University, and Technical Colleges in New South Wales *

	Full-time Enrollment					Part-time Enrollment			
Age Group	State Schools	Priv. Schools	Sydney Univ.	Teach. Col.	Total	Sydney Univ.	Univ. of Tech.	Tech. Col.	Total
14	72	23	–	–	95	–	–	–	–
15	24	14	–	–	38	–	–	10–20	10–20
16	10	7	–	–	17	–	–	20–30	20–30
17	2	4	3	1	10	0.5	0.8	15–20	15–20
18	–	1	4.5	1	6.5	0.5	0.8	10–15	10–15
19	–	–	4.5	1	5.5	0.5	0.8	10–15	10–15

* The difficulty of estimating the percentage of an age group in Sydney University and the Teachers' College turns on the fact that the students enter the University not at a fixed age but over a two-year span. The enrollment figures show that only 10 per cent of the students are on a part-time basis. The figures for the part-time enrollment in the technical colleges are estimates.

2 million) I have seen figures that indicate that the distribution of boys attending educational institutions is by age group approximately as shown in Table 9.

The university enrollment in terms of percentage of the age group reaches a maximum of 8 per cent, it will be noted. These are figures for boys only and for the Sydney metropolitan area only. The lower estimate given in Table 8 reflects the difference between boys and girls and the well-known fact that the rural areas and towns do not send as many students to a university as does an urban area. The high enrollment in part-time work leading to certificates and diplomas is evident from the figures in the last column of the table.[16] It will be noted that if one adds together the last two columns for any age group in Table 9, the total is impressive (as in the case of England — Table 7). This part-time study may be only a few hours a week at night or it may be nearly the equivalent of half-time work. It leads to certificates and diplomas based on examinations. Without the tradition of "certified education experience" to which I have referred, it would hardly succeed as it does in the British nations.

TABLE 9

Percentage of Boys of Each Age Group in School Part Time or Full Time in Sydney, New South Wales

Age Group	State Schools	Private Schools	Two Universities [*]		Total Full Time	Tech. Col. Part Time
			Full Time	Part Time		
15	29	21	—	—	50	20
16	9	14	1.1	—	24	20
17	3.5	6.5	5.5	0.5	16	30
18	1.0	1.0	6.5	1.5	8.5	30

[*] Sydney University and the New South Wales University of Technology.

The whole notion of providing at public expense for the training of boys in the trades required by an industrialized society may be regarded as an English invention of the mid-nineteenth century. The part-time training provided by taxpayers' money may be at night or in day sessions on time released by the employer. For the skilled trades the system is closely integrated with the whole British system of apprentice training. In Australia this is regulated by a mass of legislation in each state. This type of on-the-job education is particularly suitable for a society that is heavily urbanized. But in Australia the technical schools and colleges operate branches in smaller cities and in one state a specially equipped train is sent to serve as a training shop to distant towns.

The British and American mores in regard to the matter of earning a living and getting an education have been until very recently almost antithetical.[17] By and large, the American boy or girl stays in school and often goes to college while earning money on the side, particularly during the summer vacation. In the British nations the boy or girl, in the past at least, rarely earned money while in school or the university. But on leaving full-time schooling and taking a job, he or she may obtain further education on the side. This further education, however, in almost all cases is closely related to the position that is held or to the youth's vocational ambition.

Clearly there is only a thin line separating those who are earning their way through school or college by part-time work and those who have a job and are studying part time. Australians and New Zealanders have suggested to me that the difference between their system and ours on this point of part-time, full-time work is largely metaphysical. The line, while thin, is nevertheless, I believe, of real importance. The issue involved really hinges on the importance of general education or on what "degree of instruction" (to use Jefferson's phrase) is to be provided *all* the people that liberty may rest securely in their hands.

To the degree that the tax-supported education of adolescents is only a matter of developing skills or imparting knowledge relevant to a vocation, then the British method of education on-the-job may be the answer. But the experience of Australia demonstrates that an employee will usually be interested only in vocational part-time education. I know that the proponents of cultural adult education, particularly in England, will challenge this statement. But the facts and figures I have seen convince me of the truth of my generalization.

If it is important for a democracy to provide a rich cultural background for all its citizens, then the boy or girl should have his or her loyalty to the school or college and not to a job. The full-time student may profitably have work experience and many more of them from all income groups should have it. Under these conditions, education for democratic living, for developing moral and spiritual values, for an understanding of American history and ideals can continue. Once the youth's allegiance has been transferred to a job, however, his education becomes part time and it is almost certain to take the form of vocational training. Therefore, while I think we can and should look forward to a larger percentage of the youth 16 to 20 taking some part in the productive life of the nation, I think we should be unshaken in our allegiance to the American concept of full-time education.

UNITY AND DIVERSITY IN SECONDARY EDUCATION

Up to this point I have made one assumption about the future that needs further exploration.[18] I have assumed that each community in the United States would provide adequately for the education of its youth by means of tax-supported public schools locally controlled.[19] This is the characteristic pattern of secondary as well as primary education that has developed in the United States in this century. Approximately 90 per cent of those now attending high school or the equivalent are enrolled in public schools, some 8 or 9 per cent in denominational private schools, less than 2 per cent in private nonsectarian secondary schools. No tax money is used to support private secondary education.

This American pattern of education is quite different from that which has evolved in the other English-speaking nations. We have already noted the high percentage of the youth attending school in this country on a full-time basis; in addition, our pattern is characterized by the small numbers attending private schools. The absence of tax-supported denominational schools is in contrast with England and Scotland. Is this American pattern now so widely accepted that one need not argue for its preservation? Twenty or thirty years ago I think the answer would have been in the affirmative. But not so today. Any frank discussion of the future of education in the United States must recognize the existence of many powerful church leaders who do not accept the present pattern as a permanent feature of American life. One must likewise realize that while only some 10 per cent of the youth of the country now in school attend private schools, in some cities the figure is as high as 40 per cent. Furthermore, the percentage of students attending private schools is increasing in certain sections of the country.[20] Therefore I believe it of importance for all citizens to consider carefully the basic issue — the continuance of the American pattern.

I shall not detain the reader by reciting the attacks on the public schools that have taken place in the last few years (1949 to 1952). The formation in many localities of citizens' groups to defend the public schools is clear evidence of the devotion to them of a vast majority of the citizens of most towns and cities. Irresponsible attacks will certainly be warded off, and though some damage will be done, one need not fear the drastic alteration of the American pattern from violent, prejudiced criticism. But I am convinced that it is wise to discuss the fundamental criticisms of the American pattern of public education and to explore the alternative patterns which some critics favor. As a matter of convenience I shall call them the Australian and English patterns. In the one, a large proportion of the youth attending school at ages 15 to 17 is enrolled in church-connected private schools financed *without* tax support; in the other, the private school — church-connected or not — may receive tax money.[21]

Public education, like all other education and all public institutions, needs critics. But critics who believe in the continuation of the American pattern and seek to improve the schools within this framework must be clearly distinguished from those who wish to bring about an educational revolution. Therefore I think it is only fair to insist that the critics of our public schools should make clear their stand on two important points. To each one who questions the performance of our public schools, I would ask the question: "Would you like to increase the number and scope of the private schools?" If the answer is in the affirmative, I would then ask a second question: "Do you look forward to the day when tax money will directly or indirectly assist these schools?" If the answer is again in the affirmative, the lines have been clearly drawn and a rational debate on a vital issue can proceed.

Needless to say, I would find myself on the opposite side from those who answer either or both of these questions in the affirmative.[22] But what I am more concerned with in the year 1952 is that the critics of the public schools in the United States should show their colors. This is not an issue involving any single denomination. The proponents of the expansion of sectarian secondary schools are to be found in several Christian churches.[23] One of the most vocal of the critics of public high schools is a Protestant clergyman who reveals himself when he writes: "The Communist is not, as a matter of fact, much of a revolutionist. The Communist would only substitute the logical secularism of Karl Marx for the pragmatic secularism of John Dewey." If this clergyman would start off all his attacks on modern education by stating that for him secularism and communism are equal dangers, the reader would be in a better position to evaluate what he was about to read.

There are many sincere Protestants, Jews, and Catholics who believe that secondary education divorced from a de-

nominational religious core of instruction is highly unsatisfactory education.[24] They assume — erroneously, I believe —
that the tax-supported schools because they must be free of
any denominational bias cannot be concerned with moral
and spiritual values. This is essentially the point of view of
the headmasters of the Australian private schools referred to
in Chapter I. Such people, to my mind, are wrong in equating
a religious outlook with a strictly denominational viewpoint,
yet that they have a right to organize their own schools is
beyond question. The United States Supreme Court settled
the law on that point in the famous Oregon Case of 1925.[25]
But over and beyond the legal issue is the fundamental belief
in tolerance of diversity so basic to our society. I know of no
one today who wishes to suppress private schools. If there
were anyone who had such a notion, the means of putting
the idea into effect would involve such drastic state action
as to be repugnant to our fundamental ideas of liberty.[26]

But unwillingness even to consider advocating state or
national action to suppress private schools is quite a different
matter from being indifferent to their expansion. It is certainly a very different thing from acquiescing in the use of tax
money directly or indirectly for the support of private schools.

Public funds are used to assist private schools including
denominational schools in England [27] and Scotland.[28] No one
can object to an open advocacy of the adoption of the English
pattern here in the United States. Indeed, for those who believe that education divorced from denominational control is
bad education, such an advocacy would seem highly logical.[29]
It is important for every American citizen to examine this
issue as unemotionally as possible and see where he or she
stands. For there is more than one way of changing a social
pattern; we could easily drift by slow stages into a situation
where in some states the adoption of the English pattern
would be inevitable. If in a number of cities and towns the

public high schools no longer received popular support, their successful rivals — the private schools — would be logical recipients of tax money. By one method or another the present constitutional barriers against the use of public funds for religious schools would be swept aside.

During the past seventy-five years all but a few per cent of the children in the United States have attended public schools. More than one foreign observer has remarked that without these schools we never could have assimilated so rapidly the different cultures which came to North America in the nineteenth century. Our schools have served all creeds and all economic groups within a given geographic area. I believe it to be of the utmost importance that this pattern be continued. To this end the comprehensive high school deserves the enthusiastic support of the American taxpayer. The greater the proportion of our youth who fail to attend our public schools and who receive their education elsewhere, the greater the threat to our democratic unity. To use taxpayers' money to assist private schools is to suggest that American society use its own hands to destroy itself. This is the answer I must give to those who would advocate the transformation of the American pattern into that of England.

What is the basic objection to the Australian or English pattern, you may ask. Or, to put it the other way around — what are the advantages of free schools for all? To ask these questions is almost to give the answers. If one accepts the ideal of a democratic, fluid society with a minimum of class distinction, the maximum of fluidity, the maximum of understanding between different vocational groups, then the ideal secondary school is a comprehensive public high school. Of this much there can be no doubt: If one wished generation after generation to perpetuate class distinction based on hereditary status in a given society, one would certainly demand a dual system of schools; this is the case in the Province of Quebec where a majority of the people wish to perpetuate two different cultural groups. A dual system serves and helps to maintain group cleavages, the absence of a dual system does the reverse. This is particularly true of the secondary schools. Indeed, I would plead with those who insist as a matter of conscience on sending their children to denominational schools that they might limit their insistence on this type of education to the elementary years.

In terms of numbers involved, the dual nature of our present pattern may seem slight — about 92 per cent of our secondary school pupils are in public schools. In terms of a stratification of society on economic and religious lines, however, the duality is marked. In socio-economic terms we are not as far from the English "Public School" system as we sometimes like to think. Chancellor McConnell of the University of Buffalo, reporting on English education, notes the predominance of "Public School" graduates over grammar school graduates in the entrants to Oxford in 1948.[30] A half dozen of the best-known Eastern colleges in the United States would show a similar social phenomenon; they enroll something like half their students from private Protestant schools which encompass only a few per cent of an entire age group. But it is only fair to point out that these same colleges have been trying desperately hard in the last twenty-five years to attract a larger number of public high-school graduates. They aim to be national in terms of geography and representative of all income groups; that they have to some degree succeeded in moving nearer their goal is, to me, a hopeful sign.

I cannot help regretting that private schools have been established in the last twenty years in certain urban areas where a generation ago a public high school served *all* the youth of the town or city. In some of our Western cities in particular, the trend toward private education for the sons and daughters of the well-to-do has recently been pronounced, but there is no use for those of us who are committed to public high schools as schools for all to denounce or bemoan the growth of private secondary schools. The founding of a new independent school in a locality is a challenge to those connected with public education. Granted the "snob appeal" of some of these new independent schools, nevertheless I feel sure in many cases they would never have come into existence if the management of the local high school had been wiser. Education is a social process. This is a free country and people will not be pushed around by educators. What is required is for those concerned to improve the high schools; public school administrators must recognize the validity of some of the criticisms now directed against them in terms of the failure of the high school to provide adequate education for the gifted. The problem is especially acute in metropolitan areas. The success of the private school in Australian cities should be a reminder of where we may be headed.

Private schools exist and will continue to exist in the United States. Parents have the privilege of deciding whether to send their children to private or public schools. If they have doubts about the ability of secular schools to promote the growth of moral and spiritual values, then these doubts must be weighed against the advantages of a pupil's attending a free school for all denominations. Similarly, if a family questions the ability of the local high school to prepare a gifted boy or girl adequately for university work (and the question unfortunately must be raised in many communities today), the family will have to balance these misgivings against the advantage of mixing with all sorts of people while at school. It is hardly worth debating whether or not under ideal conditions in the United States all the public high schools would be so excellent that there would be no room for the private nonsectarian school. Many of those actively engaged in teaching in private schools hope that their efforts will so challenge the public schools that fewer and fewer parents will have to decide in favor of the private school for the gifted child.

Within limits, competition between private schools and public schools can be of advantage to the latter. I have used the phrase "competition within limits" advisedly, for it is difficult to run a private school without continuously recruiting students and it is difficult to recruit students without undermining public confidence in the tax-supported schools. Since the amount of money available for public education depends largely on the enthusiasm of the taxpayer, a chain reaction inimical to public education in a community may easily be started by zealous proponents of a private school. This is obvious in regard to a denominational school. If a religious group starts a school in a community, it is difficult for the promoters to avoid showing a derogatory attitude towards the rival public school. Thus even if the members of the denomination in question have no desire to receive tax money for their own private school, their criticism of the public schools may often tend to discourage the taxpayer. The same thing may happen as a result of schools that draw sons and daughters from well-to-do homes. That the growth of private schools, quite apart from the numbers enrolled, may endanger public education in a community is a fact often overlooked by those actively concerned with private education.[31]

A comparable situation does not exist as between private colleges or universities on the one hand and state or municipal institutions on the other. There has been no such attack on state universities as the recent attacks on the public secondary schools. There is no movement, as far as I am aware, to have denominational colleges or universities supported by public funds. Universities and colleges serve only a small fraction of an age group; whether state or private, they cannot, by their nature, have the unifying influence of the comprehensive high school. Some proponents of an expansion of private secondary schools have attempted to win the allegiance of private colleges by equating the function and status of a school and a college. If a private college is worth supporting, why are not *all* private schools worthwhile, it is asked. This argument misses the point at issue: namely, the value to our society of a school enrolling essentially *all* the youth of a community.

A line of rational debate becomes possible if attention is centered on a community now served only by a comprehensive high school. The question is: "Would you favor the dispersion of a considerable proportion of the present student body into a group of parallel private schools, some free and church connected, some charging fees and nonsectarian?" If your answer is yes, then a subsidiary question is whether you advocate the present Australian pattern (no tax money for the private schools) or the English pattern. But the important question is the first, for it brings to a focus the issue of the American public school as an instrument for strengthening the spirit of national unity. If a given community does not now have a comprehensive high school, or has a very poor one, the question is: "Would you try to establish a first-rate public school or a group of private schools?" The basic issue is the same.

We Americans desire to provide through our schools unity in our national life. On the other hand, we seek the diversity that comes from freedom of action and expression for small groups of citizens. We look with disfavor on any monolithic type of educational structure; we shrink from any idea of regimentation, of uniformity as to the details of the many phases of secondary education. Unity we can achieve if our public schools remain the primary vehicle for the education of our youth, and if, as far as possible, all the youth of a community attend the same school irrespective of family fortune or cultural background. Diversity in experimentation we maintain by continued emphasis on the concept of local responsibility for our schools.[32] Both these ideas are to a considerable degree novel in the development of civilization; a combination of them is to be found nowhere in the world outside of the United States.

By organizing our free schools on as comprehensive a basis as possible, we can continue to give our children an understanding of democracy. Religious tolerance, mutual respect between vocational groups, belief in the rights of the individual are among the virtues that the best of our high schools now foster. An understanding of the political machinery of our federal union, of the significance of the Anglo-Saxon tradition of the common law, of the distinction between decisions arrived at by "due process" and those obtained by social pressures and by duress, all this is now being achieved to some degree in the free tax-supported schools of this country.

What the great "Public Schools" of England accomplished for the future governing class of that nation in the nineteenth century the American high school is now attempting to accomplish for those who govern the United States, namely, all the people. Free schools where the future doctor, lawyer, professor, politician, banker, industrial executive, labor leader, and manual worker have studied and played together from the ages of 15 to 17 are a characteristic of large sections of the United States; they are an American invention. That such schools should be maintained and made even more democratic and comprehensive seems to me to be essential for the future of this republic.

Those who would grant all this but still question our free schools on religious grounds I would refer to a recent publication on "Moral and Spiritual Values in the Public Schools." [33] There is set forth in strong terms the belief of many of us that in spite of their nondenominational character, our tax-supported schools have had as a great and continuing purpose the development of moral and spiritual values.

Diversity in American secondary education will be assured if we continue to insist on the doctrine of local control. We have few restrictions on the variety of approaches to secondary education presented by our thousands of local boards. Indeed, to an outsider I should think our diversity would look like educational chaos. But this is a characteristic of our flexible decentralized concept of democracy. The time may conceivably come when a state or the Federal Government may jeopardize this concept, but as far as secondary education is concerned, I do not detect any danger signals in that direction. The National Youth Administration threat, which was real in the 1930's, has almost been forgotten.[34] In short, the answer to the question, "Can we achieve national unity through our public schools and still retain diversity?" is that we can if we so desire. My own personal answer would be that we must.

And now one final look ahead. In spite of the inadequacies of many of our high school programs and the undeveloped nature of our two-year community colleges, we have made great progress in the last twenty-five years in our attempt to provide adequate schools for *all* American youth. For the future we must endeavor to combine the British concern for training the "natural aristocracy of talents" with the American insistence on general education for *all* future citizens. If we can do that, then our industrialized society will prosper and at the same time the necessary degree of instruction will be provided for all the people so that in their hands "our liberties will remain secure."

NOTES

NOTES

Chapter I

1. The figures given in Table 1 are the best estimates I have been able to obtain but are not to be regarded as accurate within a few per cent. The English figures, calculated from data kindly supplied by the Ministry of Education, are not for the beginning of the school year but four months later (January 1). This makes the average age of a given class or year in a university somewhat higher. The New Zealand figures are for 1951 in the middle of the academic year and were kindly supplied by the Education Department; the figures for 1948 as given in the UNESCO Educational Statistics for that country are not essentially different. The figures for Scotland are taken from data kindly supplied by the Scottish Education Department (see note 14). The figures for the three Australian states were kindly supplied for South Australia by Mr. V. A. Edgeloe of the University of Adelaide; for New South Wales by Mr. H. S. Wyndham, Deputy Director General of Education; for Victoria by Mr. K. S. Cunningham, Director for the Australian Council for Educational Research.

The figures for the 17-year-old group in the three Australian states are uncertain because of the difficulty of estimating the full-time enrollment of students in the universities, teacher training colleges, and technical colleges by *age groups*. Another word of caution must be added. There are institutions giving full-time commercial and technical education in these states to pupils above the statutory leaving age, which either do not furnish statistical returns, or whose returns are not, for various reasons, included in the official compilations on which the figures in Table 1 are based.

The figures for the United States are from the *Statistical Abstract of the United States*, 1951, U. S. Department of Commerce, p. 103. The figures for 1950 by individual age groups are not yet available; for ages 14 and 15 the per cent enrolled is 95; for 16 and 17, 71 per cent. (*Current Population Reports*, U. S. Bureau of Census, Series P-20, No. 34, July 26, 1951.)

2. *The New Secondary Education*, Ministry of Education Pamphlet No. 9 (London, 1947), opens with the following sentences: "This pamphlet tells the story of a great adventure and a great investment. Part of the work is in being, as the pictures show. Most of it consists of plans for the future, but the immediate future. Here is no blue-print of Utopia. It is a description of work in progress."

The postwar years, however, have proved difficult years for expansion of education in England. The Act of 1944 provided that the age of compulsory school attendance be raised from 14 to 15 on April 1, 1947, and by a further step to 16 as soon as the Minister is satisfied that sufficient teachers and buildings are available. This "further step" it has not yet been possible to take. As a matter of fact, school attendance as such has never been compulsory in England or Wales. As the law stood until the Act of 1944 went into effect, a parent was merely required to cause his child to receive efficient elementary instruction in reading, writing, and arithmetic from the age of 5 until the end of the school term in which the child reached 14. The parent is now responsible for his child's receiving full-time education up to age 15.

For an excellent summary of the past and a look into the future of English education, the reader is referred to "A Century of British Education" by Sir John Maud (Permanent Secretary of the Ministry of Education) in *A Century of British Progress 1851–1951* (Royal Society of Arts, London, 1951).

3. *The New Secondary Education*, Ministry of Education Pamphlet No. 9 (London, 1947), p. 7.

4. "A Century of British Education," pp. 64, 66, 68, 73.

5. *The New Secondary Education*, p. 7.

6. The figures given in the text were taken from data kindly supplied by the staff of the Ministry of Education for England and Wales. Some additional figures are given below; for the selection, presentation, and interpretation of all these data I alone am responsible, attempts to reduce ten categories to four having introduced some uncertainties.

TABLE 10

Distribution of Boys in England and Wales in Various Types of Educational Programs by Percentage of Age Groups (1951)

Type of School or Curriculum	Age Groups					
	12	13	14	15	16	17
Suitable for university preparation in whole or part at public expense *	18	19	20	18	9.5	4.5
Suitable for university preparation in independent schools †	7	8	8	6	4.5	3.0
Nonacademic courses, nontechnical	72	68	66	4	—	—
Technical courses	2	4	6	4	2	1
Total in School Full Time	99+	99+	99+	32	16	8.5 ‡

* Chiefly in Grammar Schools (six-year course). (See note 7, Table 11, p. 95.)
† Private preparatory schools and the "Public Schools"; about half the number ages 14–17 enrolled in schools (mostly boarding) of the Public School type.
‡ The corresponding figure for boys *and* girls is 7.5 (see Table 1).

It will be noted from these figures that the sharp drop in school enrollment after age 14 coincides with the almost complete elimination of students in "nonacademic courses, nontechnical." In other words, the curriculum of the secondary modern schools is planned to terminate at this age. For children who proceed to the six-year Grammar School or the equivalent course in a few other schools the transition is at age 11+. For those who are attending the expensive private preparatory schools and then the Public Schools, a transition occurs at age 13+ but is not reflected in the tabulation as both types of schools are listed in the second category — "Suitable for university preparation in independent schools."

The distribution of boys at age 11 (1951) among various types of schools is interesting. Percentages of 11-year-old boys enrolled in these schools are: junior school, 23 per cent; all-age school (which enrolls to age 14), 17 per cent; secondary modern, 37 per cent; Grammar School, 12 per cent; technical, 1 per cent; independent and special, 9 per cent.

7. The educational system of England and Wales as established by the Act of 1944 can only be understood in terms of the history of secondary education in those countries. In the early nineteenth century two religious societies, one closely identified with the Church of England, established and maintained throughout the country by means of subscriptions a number of elementary schools. From 1833 to 1870 a system of elementary schools was managed and maintained by several private organizations with some grants from Parliament and with the aid of fees. In 1870 by Act of Parliament locally elected School Boards were required to provide elementary schools in areas where the private schools (called Voluntary Schools) were insufficient; these schools (Board Schools) were supported by local taxes, Parliamentary grants, and fees. There was almost no provision for secondary education at public expense in England or Wales until the end of the century. The Education Act of 1902 marks the beginning of a system of publicly supported elementary and secondary education. F. Smith in *A History of English Elementary Education* (London, 1931) writes: "The Education Act of 1902 brought administrative order where there had been chaos, and set up an organized system of elementary, secondary and technical education." The local School Boards were abolished as being a block to the development of free secondary education. The county (and county borough) councils were given the power to provide education locally. Instead of 2,500 School Boards, about three hundred county councils became the new local education authorities.

"The Act of 1902, like most Education Acts, presented many features of compromise," writes S. J. Curtis in his *History of Education in Great Britain* (London, 1948, Chapter IX). ". . . It created local education authorities empowered to coordinate elementary and higher education, and provided what at the time was described as 'the ladder from the elementary school to the university' because it rendered possible the award of scholarships for promising pupils from the elementary school. It gave the denominational schools a definite place in the system and ensured that the pupils in these schools received an education up to the standard of that provided in the council schools . . . The . . . Act did not go so far as to create a national system of education, but it laid the foundation on which others would be able to build."

The principle of public money flowing to private denominational schools was established by the Act of 1902. The bitter controversy which centered around this feature will be referred to later (Chapter III, note 27, page 145). The ultimate results of this legislation have been summarized as follows: "(a) The establishment and rapid development of secondary (grammar) schools wholly provided and maintained by local education authorities. (b) The granting of financial assistance by local education authorities to a number of secondary (grammar) schools already in existence — in some cases existing secondary schools were completely taken over by the local education authorities. (c) The coordination and further development of technical instruction . . . (d) The establishment of a number of training colleges for teachers. . . ." (*A Guide to the Educational System of England and Wales*, Ministry of Education Pamphlet No. 2, London, 1945, pp. 50–51.)

There were thus two categories of public elementary schools: the *provided* or council school where the local education authority had complete responsibility, both financial and otherwise; and the *nonprovided* or voluntary school where the provision and upkeep of the school buildings as well as the appointment of teachers was the responsibility of the school managers, though the secular instruction was under the control of the local education authority. Religious instruction might, and almost invariably was, given in the voluntary school but was prohibited in the council school.

The Local Education Authority was responsible for the maintenance costs in both types of schools; that is, the salaries of teachers, the cost of educational material and equipment, and so on. "This system, known as the 'dual system' with its legal safeguards and divided responsibilities, gave rise to much complication in administration and seriously retarded educational progress. Not only had the local education authority no effective power to alter the organization of a voluntary school . . . but the denominations concerned — mainly the Church of England and the Roman Catholic Church — found it quite impossible to finance the improvements which were necessary. . .

"In the field of the grammar schools there was no dual system as such, the relationship between governing bodies and local education authorities being much looser and less formal. . . The 1944 Act has dealt with the problem of both voluntary elementary and voluntary grammar schools by offering all of them (except those which become special agreement schools) the choice of two alternatives. . ." (*A Guide to the Educational System of England and Wales*, pp. 25–26.)

The alternatives may be summarized for American readers as follows: (1) A "controlled school" is a private school in which the board of trustees (managers or governors in England) have given up their power of appointing teachers to the local education authority except for a proportion of the teachers who may give denominational instruction for two periods a week, and (2) an "aided school" is a private school still under the management of the trustees, who in return agree to meet half the cost of alterations, improvements, and external repairs. All the costs of education in both cases are paid from the local taxes and Parliament grant through the Local Education Authority. There is no transfer of ownership in either case. The Local Education Authority names one third of the Board of Trustees (managers or governors) in the case of the aided schools and two thirds in the case of the controlled schools. The effect of these new arrangements on religious instruction is considered in a note to Chapter III (note 27, page 145). (The so-called "special agreement schools" may be regarded as special cases of aided schools.) One further complication is the existence of direct grants from the Ministry of Education to a few private grammar schools (or their equivalent) on condition that a proportion of their students (usually 25 per cent) should be admitted from public elementary schools essentially without payment of fees.

This option was open to the "Public Schools" but has not been taken advantage of by any of the famous boarding schools. The Manchester Grammar School is an example of a direct grant school. In general the Church of England schools are either independent (the "Public Schools"), direct grant, aided, or controlled; the Roman Catholic Schools are either independent, direct grant, or aided.

The following estimates as to enrollment of boys in the various types of schools (January 1951) are based on data kindly supplied by the staff of the Ministry of Education.

TABLE 11

Percentages of Age Groups (Boys) Enrolled in Schools of Various Types

| Type of School | Age Group | |
	14	17
Independent, all types (no public money)	9	3.8
Direct Grant (some free places)	2.4	0.7
Voluntary (aided, controlled)		
Modern	11.0	—
Grammar	5.4	1.3
Technical	0.3	—
Other	0.1	—
	16.8	1.3
County (Local Education Authority)		
Modern	53.0	—
Grammar	11.0	2.7
Technical	5.5	0.1
Other	1.3	0.1
	71.1	2.9

It will be clear from these figures that while a large percentage of the boys (and the same is true of girls) aged 14 attend schools completely under public management, the same is not true for age 17. Here only about half of those enrolled are in what American educators would call public schools; the others are in schools more or less under private management. (For the relation of this management to various denominations, see Chapter III, note 27, page 145.)

The relation of the independent and direct grant schools to the universities is illustrated by the following figures published in the London *Economist* for May 24, 1952:

"The winning of an open scholarship at Oxford or Cambridge is still the crown of a schoolboy's career. There are other universities; and there are, nowadays, many other forms of award from the state and from local education authorities. . . But the scholarships and exhibitions awarded by the Oxford and Cambridge colleges after competitive examination still stand in a class entirely by themselves as a test of the merits of the schools and their scholars. . . The total of awards in the two universities was 854; of these, 841 were won from schools which fall into one of the recognised categories, as follows: —

	OXFORD		CAMBRIDGE	
	No. of Awards	Per Cent	No. of Awards	Per Cent
Independent	212	56.25	227	48.9
Direct Grant	51	13.5	75	16.2
Maintained	114	30.25	162	34.9

" 'Independent' schools are those which are entirely self-supporting; 'maintained' schools belong to the state system; 'direct grant' schools are an intermediate category."

This analysis, it will be noted, does not distinguish between the aided schools, the controlled schools, or the county schools — they are all treated as belonging to the state system. A list of the schools which won eight or more places in 1951–1952 is headed by a direct-grant school — Manchester Grammar School — with three "Public Schools" — Winchester, Eton, and St. Paul's (a day school in London) — next in that order.

The financial and administrative arrangements under the Act of 1944 are such as to give 146 county and county borough councils the power to levy local taxes (rates) for education as well as other services. On the average, about 60 per cent of the costs of the elementary and secondary maintained schools (aided and controlled as well as county schools) are supplied by funds voted by Parliament annually, and 40 per cent from the local taxes. But in communities where the capacity to pay taxes is low, the Parliamentary grant may supply as much as 90 per cent of the funds required. Of the 146 local education authorities, 84 are County-Borough Councils (of which the London County Council is the largest) and 62 county councils. Omitting certain complications arising in some counties because of large towns, one may say that the same elected body controls the schools as controls the police, the sewage system, and other local services. The contrast with the American tradition of having the local school boards usually independent of the town or city authorities is worthy of notice.

The local education authority appoints a chief educational officer who is to some degree parallel to a city school superintendent in the United States but with far less power. (There are only 146 such officers, it must be noted, in all of England and Wales.) There is an educational committee appointed by the council to have direct concern with educational matters. But the management of each school by a special board of governors or managers is an essential element in the English tradition and is carried over from the voluntary schools to the county schools. The details of the curriculum in each school are largely determined by the governors and the teachers with the consent of the local education authorities (in maintained schools). It is perhaps fair to say that in England no group of citizens has as much power as that exercised by the local school boards in the United States; further, no one person has the range of responsibility of an American school superintendent. Whereas in the

United States we stress the idea of local control by the citizens, the English stress the idea of the autonomy of each secondary school, thus carrying over into "public education" much of the spirit of independence of private education.

The central authority for Education in England and Wales is the Ministry of Education. The political head of the Department is the Minister of Education. The Department is staffed by a body of permanent civil servants — with the Permanent Secretary at their head. "The system of Education in England and Wales judged from the point of view of organisation and administration differs in three main respects from the systems to be found in many other countries. These characteristic features are the decentralisation of educational administration; the prominent part played by voluntary agencies; and the freedom of teachers from official direction on questions relating to curricula, syllabuses of instruction and methods of teaching." (*A Guide to the Educational System of England and Wales*, p. 5.)

I am indebted to Sir John Maud, Permanent Secretary of the Ministry, and his staff for valuable information concerning secondary education in England today. But I alone am responsible for this summary of a complex situation and the contrasts drawn between English and American methods of financing and administering secondary schools. The reader is referred for further details to the sources quoted above and also *The New Secondary Education*, Ministry of Education Pamphlet No. 9, 1947; and H. C. Dent, *The Education Act of 1944* (London, 1944).

8. *Time* magazine for February 4, 1952, carried a story entitled "Ordeal in London" describing how "32,000 little Londoners, aged 10½ to 11½" were taking examinations that month "as if they thought their very lives depended on their answers." The story (here reprinted from *Time*, February 4 Issue, Copyright Time Inc., 1952) continues:

"The examinations they were taking were the awesome 'selection tests' — Britain's new way of finding out just what sort of secondary education each child should have. If he does well, he will win a coveted 'place' in one of the 'grammar' schools, and there he will get a solid academic education that may eventually lead him to a university. If he does not do so well, he will be sent to a 'central' or 'secondary technical' school where he will spend more time on vocational training. The bottom 60% of the children will end up in a 'secondary modern' school. There, formal academic training is at a minimum.

"SO WORKED UP. The selection system started in 1944, when the British government decided that every child should get a free secondary education. Before that, parents paid the bill, and most children merely stayed on in elementary schools until they could legally drop out at 14. Now all children must go on to secondary school at eleven. Since too few grammar schools exist, the government has had to set up a rigid system of selection. But by last week, as the London exams fell due, some Britons were asking whether the system is really worth while.

"Teachers were willing to admit that the tests could winnow out the bright and the quick. But they still did not pick out the hard-working or the talented. They gave no quarter to the late bloomers, made no allowances for children who happened to be overwrought during the exam. Cried one parent last week: 'The test gets the child so worked up. My Patricia went out of the house white as a sheet, and couldn't eat any breakfast.' Added another: 'It's terrible to think that what a boy does at eleven will govern his whole life.'

". . . Last week the controversy boiled up anew when A. G. Hughes, chief inspector in the Education Officers' Department of the London County Council, published a book with some severe words for the whole tripartite idea.

" 'It is very doubtful,' said he, 'whether on the basis of tests we ought ever to dare to decide, at the age of ten, whether an intelligent boy with practical aptitude is destined to become an academic scientist via a grammar school or a practical engineer via a secondary technical school. . . Is it right to segregate. . . dull and bright, bookish-minded and practical-minded pupils. . . during the impressionable and formative period of adolescence? . . . Is it right to determine the type of education so early without reference to the changes of interest that so often develop during adolescence?'

"Apparently some Britons thought it was not right. The trouble is that until the nation can afford enough 'comprehensive schools' to accommodate every one, eleven-year-olds will have to go through the same ordeal that hit the little Londoners last week."

In an article in *The Listener* for April 17, 1952, entitled "Plight of the Middle Class," John Beavan points out how hard it is for the intellectual worker in England to enjoy even the amenities which he needs to carry on his work. "His greatest concern is education," he continues. "The most intelligent children can almost always get through to grammar school and university. But suppose your child is just average. If you can afford only the state education, he is going to finish his day school at fifteen and to be socially de-classed by his education at a time when competition for middle-class jobs is fiercer than it has ever been.

"The English public schools are not merely institutions which give a child a class privilege as long as he lives. They produce scholars as well as gentlemen, and most boys emerge from them with the characteristics that are most highly esteemed in this country. A man who has been to such a school himself will make appalling sacrifices to give his son the same advantages, and if even with such sacrifice he still cannot manage it, he feels he has failed in his duty as a parent."

It is not only the cost of maintaining a boy in an English "Public School" that drains a family's resources. The private schools preparing for the public school (often boarding schools for boys aged 8 to 14) are even more expensive.

Sir Richard Livingstone has contrasted the American and British patterns of education in an address over the British Broadcasting Company's network (printed in *The Listener* for July 3, 1952, p. 17). He sums up as follows:

"American education is immensely interesting and full of the vitality and experiment characteristic of the country. Contact with it is stimulating apart from any lessons it may have for us. It is, however, important not to learn the wrong things from it but to study it in the spirit of Polonius' admirable maxim: 'Take each man's censure, but reserve thy judgment.' "

An editorial in the same issue commenting on this address notes, "It is not easy for British and American citizens to understand each other's systems of education"; and concludes as follows:

"The real difference between education in the two countries springs from two factors: first, that the United States is a richer country than ours; second, that it has a different historical and political tradition. In this country the notion that Jack is not as good as his master dies hard. At the moment thousands of members of the professional and other middle classes are drawing on their savings to give their sons an expensive education. To the average American parent of the same class the idea of doing so would appear fantastic. How long we shall cling to these sacrifices on the altar of tradition no one can say. But, other things being equal, we are more likely to come round to the American way of thinking than they are to ours."

9. The tradition of the English grammar school was maintained in colonial America by such institutions as the Roxbury Latin School in Roxbury (now a part of the city of Boston), and the Boston Latin School. Both institutions are over three hundred years old and provide a six-year classical course of study today much as they have for centuries. The former was originally called a grammar school in Roxbury and was managed by a board of trustees which still functions. The Boston Latin School became a part of the Boston public school system and does not retain any board of trustees. If the expenses of the Roxbury Latin School were now paid by the state and municipal authorities, its status would be closely parallel to an "aided" or "controlled" English grammar school. (See note 7.)

10. One of the consequences of the different historical developments of education in the two Kingdoms of Great Britain is the diametrically opposed uses of the adjective "public." A public school in Scotland is a school supported by public funds and nowadays with certain exceptions free. The "Public Schools" of England have, of course, been patronized by Scotch families but there seems to have been little tendency to transfer the English nomenclature across the border.

The difference in the development of education in England and Scotland reflects the differences in the religious history of the two nations. From the Reformation on, the Scots were Presbyterians and in spite of the attempts to fasten episcopacy on them and the feud between two rival church organizations the nation may be said to have been culturally homogeneous. Certainly so as compared with England, which from the time of the Clarendon Code (1661) on was divided bitterly into adherents of the Established Church and the dissenters or nonconformists. As a consequence, all education in England until late in the nineteenth century was organized around voluntary religious groups. In Scotland education from early times was a local responsibility and after the Reformation when Kirk and State were nominally one, public schools were also essentially church schools. (As to the present status of denominational schools in Scotland, see Chapter III, note 28, page 149.) The similarity between the attitudes of the seventeenth-century Scottish and New England theocracies towards education is evident.

11. Alexander Morgan, *Rise and Progress of Scottish Education* (Edinburgh: Oliver and Boyd, 1927), p. 43.

12. *Ibid.*, pp. 44–46.

13. *Ibid.*, p. 73.

14. The Act of 1872 laid the groundwork for all later developments in Scottish education. As early as 1878 local school boards were empowered to levy taxes for the upkeep of secondary schools. The Act of 1918 represented the first and most important step forward in secondary education. Primary

education was recognized as normally ending at 12 and free intermediate and secondary schooling was made mandatory for all children able to profit by it.

The Advisory Council on Education in Scotland in its report on Secondary Education dated October 1946 (Scottish Education Department, Edinburgh, 1947, p. 180) has this to say about the tradition of Scottish education:

"Our educational system is not always understood south of the Border. Any temporary opprobrium that may in England attach to 'Council' schools [that is, county schools] does not exist in Scotland. There is no native tradition of 'public' or boarding or preparatory schools. Our public schools are day schools, whether primary or secondary. These are not nineteenth-century innovations, but have an ancient national tradition behind them, dating from the Reformation or long before. Some of our day secondary schools in the burghs have many centuries of continuous history, having unbroken records of up to eight hundred years. Over 97 per cent. of the children in Scotland attend schools under the direct control of the education authorities or receiving grants from the Secretary of State. It may fairly be claimed therefore that the Scottish system of education is both democratic and national.

"Some of our witnesses have expressed the regret, which is widely felt, at the decrease in size and prestige of many of our rural schools, and that 'the country schoolmaster, with all that he once meant to the community, is rapidly disappearing.' Here it must be plainly stated that education authorities have to be realistic. Just as the decay of rural Scotland in the past century was due to well-understood economic causes, and not at all to the lack of good education in the parish schools, the rehabilitation of rural Scotland could not be effected by setting up in every small area fully equipped and adequately staffed schools. None are more anxious than those who have the welfare of Scottish education at heart — Department, authorities and teachers alike — that the rural areas of Scotland should have a large and thriving population. But this can be achieved only through a widely planned national policy, in which education will take a responsible and generous part. Such, it must be recognised, is the spirit and the promise of the 1945 Act."

The responsibility for the local provision of education now rests with the "Education Authorities" which consist of the town councils of Glasgow, Edinburgh, Aberdeen, and Dundee, the county councils of 29 counties and the joint county councils of certain other counties. These authorities are thus very similar to what in England are known as the Local Education Authorities and they operate through an education committee in much the same manner. The Government Department charged with the general direction of education in Scotland is the Scottish Education Department. It is the function of this department to see that the local Education Authorities discharge the duty laid upon them by law of providing for the educational needs of the residents of their area.

Unlike the situation in England, all but a few per cent of the children attend tax-supported schools managed by the local Education Authority. The problems presented today by the independent Grammar Schools of England have never existed in Scotland because of the different religious history of the two Kingdoms. There are a few grant-aided private schools in essentially the same status as the direct-grant schools of England. But since 1918 most

TABLE 12

Scottish Educational Pattern (1951)

Distribution of Boys and Girls between Schools and Other Educational Institutions on a Full-Time and Part-Time Basis in Scotland (assuming no military service before completion of course)

Percentage of Age Group Enrolled

Age Group	Primary and Secondary Education — State † and State-aided Voluntary ‡ Schools				Full-Time Further Education *			Total Full Time	Part-Time Education
	Primary and Special	Secondary — Junior Courses ††	Secondary — Senior Courses	Independent Schools	Further Education Institutions	Teachers Training Centers **	Universities		
10	96.8	–	0.2	2.0	–	–	–	99.0	–
11	85.5	4.0	7.5	2.0	–	–	–	99.0	–
12	28.0	57.0	12.0	2.0	–	–	–	99.0	–
13	3.6	74.6	19.0	2.0	–	–	–	99.0	–
14	2.3	75.7	19.0	2.0	–	–	–	99.0	–
15	1.6	18.0	14.0	1.7	2.0	–	–	37.3	27.5
16	–	1.0	9.2	1.1	2.6	–	–	13.9	28.5
17	–	–	6.3	0.4	1.8	–	1.0	9.5	29.0
18	–	–	2.3	0.2	2.5	0.5	3.0	8.5	25.0
19	–	–	0.5	–	2.8	0.7	4.0	8.0	25.0
20	–	–	–	–	1.8	0.7	4.0	6.5	25.0
21	–	–	–	–	1.3	0.7	3.0	5.0	Not available
22	–	–	–	–	0.5	0.5	2.0	3.0	
23	–	–	–	–	0.2	0.1	0.8	1.1	
24	–	–	–	–	–	–	0.3	0.3	

* Excludes girls training as nurses.
† About 85 per cent for Protestant and about 15 per cent for Roman Catholic pupils.
‡ State-aided voluntary schools take less than 1 per cent of age group.
** Includes University graduates training as teachers. Men teachers are normally graduates.
†† About 20 per cent of pupils attending Junior Secondary Courses take modified courses.

of the private schools have become "transferred schools," the buildings now being the property of the Education Authority and the management of the school in the hands of a School Management Committee, at least one member of which is of the same religious belief as that of the parents whose children attend the school. (See also Chapter III, note 28, page 149.) In the year ending July 31, 1951, there were 3,125 public schools with an average attendance of 783,088 pupils; 23 grant-aided schools with an average attendance of 12,211 pupils; and 200 independent schools (receiving no public money) attended by about 20,000 pupils (2.4 per cent of the total). (*Education in Scotland*, Scottish Education Department, Edinburgh DE10335/1, August 1951, p. 2.)

The figures in Table 12 were supplied by the Scottish Education Department. They are for both sexes. For boys only, the university enrollment is higher (5.5 for 19 and 20 year olds).

Attendance at school is compulsory to age 15. The primary school is attended by children from the age of 5 to 12. There are two types of secondary schools: those providing courses normally extending for three years (junior secondary schools), and those providing courses of five or six years (senior secondary schools). While some schools are purely junior or purely senior secondary schools, others are of the "comprehensive" type in which both junior and senior courses are offered. When a pupil has completed the primary course he is promoted at ages 11+ to 12+ to the secondary stage. "For purposes of promotion, pupils are graded according to their fitness to profit from a three year or from a five year secondary course, and, within each of these, from the more or less difficult courses provided. This assessment is based on evidence derived from class records over the last three years of the primary course and from the results of standardised intelligence tests and attainment tests in English and arithmetic, according to the Promotion Scheme approved for the area by the Secretary of State." (*Education in Scotland*, p. 6.)

The five or six year course includes English, history or geography, arithmetic, art and music, all studied throughout the course; in addition the course includes languages other than English, mathematics, science, history or geography, but not necessarily studied for all five or six years. The Scottish Leaving Certificate is awarded by the Scottish Education Department to those completing the senior course.

15. John Rodgers, *The Old Public Schools of England* (London, 1938), p. 32.

16. G. M. Trevelyan, *English Social History* (Longmans, New York, 1944), pp. 519–520, quoted here by permission of Longmans, Green & Co., Inc.

17. The data presented in Table 2 were obtained from the following sources: For South Australia from Mr. V. A. Edgeloe; for New South Wales from Mr. H. S. Wyndham, Deputy Director of Education; for Victoria, calculations from the data supplied by the Australian Council for Educational Research. (See note 1.) Since the official data for Victoria are given in numbers by age groups and classes for tax-supported schools but classes only for private schools, there are difficulties of interpretation. The following factual data are therefore to be noted:

Total enrollment in Form V for tax-supported secondary schools, 1,763; for Roman Catholic schools, 1,069; for Protestant Private Schools, 2,008; for Form VI, tax supported, 601; Roman Catholic, 485; Protestant Private Schools, 1,255. If one takes Form V as corresponding to age 16 and the size of the age group as approximately 26,000, and treats the data accordingly, figures similar to those given in Table 2 are obtained. I have omitted all enrollments in the universities, teaching training institutions, and technical colleges from these calculations as data on the age distribution of the enrollments in these institutions are not readily available.

18. From a letter written to me by the head of one of the leading Church of England schools in Australia.

19. Data kindly furnished me by Mr. Wyndham, Deputy Director of Education of New South Wales, are summarized in Table 13 and show the distribution of students between different types of schools in that state.

TABLE 13

Distribution (Percentage of Age Group) of Young People in New South Wales as between Different Types of Schools (1950)

Age Group	Primary State	High, Jr. High and Int. High	Jr. Tech. Home Science Dist. Rural (State)	Other	Total State	Private School	Total in School
11	76	—	—	—	76	24	100
12	46	18	9	5	78	22	100
13	14	31	20	9	75	25	100
14	3	32	24	13	72	23	95
15	—	16	5	3	24	14	38
16	—	8	2	—	10	8	18

These figures are in one sense incomplete because both Catholic and Protestant private schools are lumped together. Actually, the two types of schools draw on different socio-economic groups and, of course, have quite different traditions. The figures available in Victoria (see Table 2 in text) show that the Protestant private schools keep their students until graduation while the Catholic schools lose them about as do the state schools. Indeed, in Victoria, because of transfer from state schools, some private schools have more students age 15 than at age 11. If the same factors are at work in New South Wales, the drop in the private school enrollment between age groups 14 and 15 must represent the loss of some 75 per cent of the enrollment of the Catholic schools.

The various types of post-primary schools in New South Wales are divided into two: (1) those to which admission is determined by competition, (2) those to which admission is not determined competitively. In the first group are all the high schools (general, technical, and home science). In the noncompetitive group are the junior technical and commercial schools and the home science schools. Parents are asked to indicate the post-primary school which they desire their child to enter but are warned that their statement only makes the child a candidate for the school named and his final admission is determined by the Department of Education. The successful candidate for admission to a high school in the metropolitan area must attend the high school in the area in which he lives. The break between primary and secondary school comes at the average age of 13.2 (at the end of the sixth educational year). In considering the claims of primary school pupils for enrollment at post-primary schools, the Intelligence Quotient is an important factor. For this reason, arrangements are made for the testing of all pupils in departmental schools before the end of their primary school career.

The general high schools provide the full five-year course to the Leaving Certificate Examinations. In common with other schools, they include in the courses physical education, English, mathematics, a science, music, art and needlework for girls, and history, geography or social studies. Pupils admitted to them must take at least one foreign language (usually French or German).

After the vacancies in the type of high school just described have been filled, pupils who have been unsuccessful in the competition are considered for junior or intermediate high schools. A course similar to that provided by the general high school may be obtained at such schools but one gathers that other courses of a more technical nature predominate; the number of those who proceed from these schools to a university is less than from the general high school. Taking the general high, the intermediate and junior high together, they account for an enrollment of nearly 35 per cent of the age group 14 (as shown in Table 12). At age 16 it appears that only the general high schools enroll an appreciable number: they account for 8 per cent of the age group.

The home science high schools and the technical high schools do not cater primarily to those who are interested in university work. Though the five-year course does provide subjects which may comprise the requirements of the Leaving Certificate Examination, the technical high schools emphasize instruction in technical subjects such as wood and metal working. The courses do enable students to enter the University of Sydney or the New South Wales University of Technology, and a few take advantage of this.

The noncompetitive schools (junior technical, home science, and rural schools) do not prepare for the Leaving Certificate Examination. They offer a general course without a foreign language. Together they enroll 24 per cent of the age group at age 14 (Table 12, column 4). But only a few per cent of the age group are enrolled at 16.

The admission to the competitive schools is based on (1) the child's cumulative primary school record; (2) the recommendation of the school principal; (3) results of intelligence tests.

Hostels are provided for high school pupils in connection with a number of the high schools in towns outside of Sydney. Bursaries are provided by state funds and awarded on the basis of a competitive examination on English, mathematics, and a combined paper in history and geography, topics studied in the last year of the primary school. These bursaries are awarded only if the income is below £485 (for three dependents), and pay £12 for students living at home, £50 for students living away from home. Combined with the hostels, these arrangements provide an opportunity for the ambitious family and bright boy or girl from a rural area to proceed with high school education.

The Intermediate Certificate Examination is important because it measures the progress of the student and also because the standing of a student on this examination determines the possibility of a bursary or scholarship. In New South Wales the examination comes in the ninth educational year (third of secondary education, approximately at age 15.0). The candidate must present himself for examination in not less than six nor more than eight subjects drawn from certain groups. These permit a number of combinations outside of such an orthodox list as English, physics, history (or social studies), algebra, geometry, French, Latin. For example, the following would appear to be permitted: English, social studies (or history), physiology and hygiene, combined physics and chemistry, home economics and needlecraft — or substituting for the last two, woodwork or metal work. Such a combination corresponds to the courses offered in the technical high schools.

It is important to note that in recent years some approved schools have been allowed to give their own examinations for the leaving certificate. These internal examinations follow the same rules and correspond to the same syllabi as the external.

In New South Wales it is stated in the official pamphlet of the Department of Education that "The pupil returning to school after qualifying for the award of the Intermediate Certificate should have some clear indication as to what he or she aims to achieve by doing so. Consideration needs to be paid to the requirements for University Matriculation and Technical College Diploma Entrance . . ." *Guide to Past Primary Courses Examinations and Scholarships 1951* (Sydney, 1951), p. 49.

20. *Education Today and Tomorrow* by Hon. H. G. R. Mason, Minister of Education, New Zealand (Wellington, 1944), p. 8, giving the statement of the Right Honorable P. Fraser, Minister of Education in 1939 in his annual report.

21. *Education for All American Youth*, Educational Policies Commission of the National Education Association of the United States and the American Association of School Administrators (Washington, D. C., 1944). A new revised edition entitled *Education for All American Youth, A Further Look* was published in May 1952.

22. Address to the Senate of the University of New Zealand, Christchurch, August 21, 1951, by the Honorable Sir David Smith, Chancellor of the University. On page 20 the Chancellor quotes Dr. Beeby, Director of Education for New Zealand, as follows:

"Dr. Beeby considers that we have gone a considerable distance towards the American idea of higher education though we have tended to retain the internal structure and the methods of teaching of the European university. He thinks that this fact is the source of some of the dissatisfaction of university teachers with the standard of their students."

As to the increase in the holding power of the schools, the figures in

Table 14 kindly supplied by Mr. A. E. Campbell, Director of the New Zealand Council for Educational Research, are of interest. The school leaving age was raised from 14 to 15 in 1944.

TABLE 14

Percentage of Age Group Enrolled in Full-Time Education in New Zealand 1931–1951

Age	1931	1939	1949	1951
14	63.9	70.5	100	100
15	37.6	40.5	58.8	60.0
16	19.1	19.8	31.6	31.0
17	9.0	8.9	14.9	14.0

23. The judgment about earlier specialization in the British schools is, of course, relative. It must be viewed in the light of the absence of the equivalent of the American college in any British nation. (See Chapter II; and especially note 31, page 125.) What appear to be largely absent in the Australian schools from which students may enter a university are considerable periods of time devoted to history, geography, the social studies, music and the arts, though these subjects are being increasingly emphasized. What is *present* is more striking, namely, a continuation of the emphasis on foreign languages, mathematics, and for those with a scientific bent, physics and chemistry. The future engineer, scientist, or doctor has to begin the study of science rather than a second language at school at age 14 or 15.

24. I may have overemphasized the extent of the revolution in New Zealand or placed too much stress on the curriculum changes, for at the same time two full years of secondary schooling were added to the requirement for apprenticeship to a trade. Further, the increased prosperity of New Zealand may have been a factor in increasing the enrollment of 16- and 17-year-olds, though full employment may also work in the opposite direction.

As to the curriculum changes, Mr. Campbell informs me that in 1943 "of all pupils in secondary schools 22 per cent were following professional or general courses with two foreign languages, 27 per cent with one foreign language. In 1951 these percentages had dropped to 8 and 21." A large change, but perhaps not a revolution.

25. See Table 2, page 16. The figures for private and public school enrollment for New Zealand are for 1948, taken from the chart prepared by UNESCO on School Education Statistics. The figures for July 1950, kindly supplied by Mr. Campbell, are for the over-all secondary school enrollment — 59,046 — of which 48,535 are in public schools, 6,187 in Catholic schools, and 4,324 in Protestant schools. Thus some 10.5 per cent of the total secondary school population was enrolled in Catholic schools, 7.3 per cent in Protestant private schools.

26. In presenting an account of New Zealand education to the audience at the University of Virginia, I erroneously oversimplified the picture. The

accounts of my speech which were printed in the New Zealand papers failed to emphasize the contrast of the role of the *Protestant* private school in Australia and New Zealand. As a consequence, an item appeared in a Catholic paper, *The Zealandia* (Auckland), for March 6, 1952, which I quote in part here to right the record:

"The president of Harvard University, Dr. James B. Conant, paid a visit to this country last year during a meeting of the Senate of the University of New Zealand. We have no immediate record of his guides or informants during whatever studies he made of our educational system; but we have every reason to suppose that these suffered from a partial blindness which they communicated to the American visitor. Such is the only conclusion possible in charity, from the *Christchurch Press* report (February 28) of Dr. Conant's three Page-Barbour lectures at the University of Viriginia, delivered early last month.

". . . he delivered himself of a series of observations which Catholics with any knowledge at all of their own school arrangements will recognise as downright absurd. . . . we give the report as it appeared in the southern daily . . .

"The role of private schools was mentioned with interest. Nowhere in the world did the private Protestant school flourish as in several Australian States. In two large States there were more sixteen to seventeen-year-old students in private schools than in tax-supported schools. '*Yet right across the Tasman Sea in New Zealand the role of the private school is negligible both in terms of numbers and of influence,*' Dr. Conant said. . . .

" '. . . There are insufficient wealthy people in New Zealand to support more than one or two boarding schools; hence there is only a trace of the dual system of education,' . . .

" 'Only a trace,' he said. Of the thirty-one names which appeared on the lists of University scholarship winners from New Zealand's secondary schools last year, nine were from private schools (five of them Catholics) — practically 30 per cent; not, by any figures, an insignificant 'trace.' It is hard to understand just why Dr. Conant should have looked only at Protestant schools when he evaluated the 'dual system,' with the Catholic colleges and convents that are found in every diocese of the country; . . .

"Maybe, by Harvard standards, there are 'insufficient wealthy people' in New Zealand to permit private schools to flourish; yet Catholics have built a complete system utterly disregarded by Dr. Conant, not out of their wealth but out of their spirit of resolution and sacrifice, not for the sons and daughters of the wealthy alone but for all Catholic children without discrimination. Wealth is not the only pre-requisite for the existence of a private school system; other values are needed as well — but there is no trace of them in the reports of Dr. Conant's observations.

"In general, it may be noted that the architects of our modern educational world often fall into the trap of judging money, big buildings, lavish equipment and high salaries as the warp and woof of which education is woven. They tend to neglect the things of mind and heart and character and soul, which the private (in our case, religious) school holds in first importance, and which are in fact the most valuable contribution any school can make to the building of a nation. . . .

"Dr. Conant's misinterpretation of the New Zealand school system on its highly important private side is bad enough; far more dangerous still is the philosophy evident behind his observations."

Clearly I failed in my first account of New Zealand to do justice to the influence if not the extent of Catholic education in that country. There are nineteen Anglican schools (five for Maoris), seven Presbyterian, and two Methodist schools in New Zealand. Some of the Anglican boys' schools have large boarding departments and are in many ways the New Zealand counterpart of the English Public Schools and their Australian equivalents. The enrollment figures given on page 23 clearly show, however, the difference in the position of the Protestant private school for the education of adolescents in New Zealand on the one hand, and New South Wales, South Australia, and Victoria on the other.

The religious composition of the population in New Zealand and Australia is shown in Table 15.

TABLE 15

Distribution by Percentage of Population of New Zealand and Australia According to Principal Religious Groups *

Denomination	New Zealand	Australia
Church of England	37	39
Catholic	14	21
Presbyterian	23	10
Methodist	8	12

* Figures are taken from the 1945 and 1947 Census reports. Percentages are approximate.

27. Figures for ages 14 through 17 from 1910 through 1940 are taken from the *Statistical Abstract of the United States,* 1951, U. S. Department of Commerce, p. 103. The 1890 figure was calculated from figures obtained in *Eleventh Census of the United States,* Vol. 2. The 1900 figure was obtained from *Thirteenth Census of the United States,* Vol. 1, p. 1103, as was the 1910 figure for ages 10–14. Figures for ages 10–13 for the years 1920 and 1930 were based on statistics from *Statistical Abstract of the United States,* 1951, p. 103. Figures for ages 10–13 for 1940 and 1950 were given in *Current Population Reports,* U. S. Bureau of Census, Series P-20, No. 34, July 26, 1951. Some pertinent data are given in *Equal Educational Opportunity for Youth: A National Responsibility,* American Council on Education, 1930, p. 23; but these figures seem inconsistent with data from Table 3 based on appropriate Census reports.

28. The data for separate states *now* available are shown here in Table 16 and are taken from the U. S. Bureau of Census: *Sixteenth Census of the United States,* 1940, *Population, Characteristics by Age,* Parts 2, 3, and 4, Table 15.

TABLE 16

Percentage of School Attendance at Age 16 (1940)

Alabama	65.4	Louisiana	65.0	Ohio	85.8
Arizona	70.3	Maine	73.9	Oklahoma	77.1
Arkansas	64.5	Maryland	65.8	Oregon	84.4
California	91.0	Massachusetts	82.3	Pennsylvania	83.9
Colorado	78.6	Michigan	80.9	Rhode Island	69.7
Connecticut	81.5	Minnesota	76.6	So. Carolina	62.5
Delaware	72.7	Mississippi	66.0	So. Dakota	76.9
D.C.	83.7	Missouri	70.1	Tennessee	61.6
Florida	69.7	Montana	83.4	Texas	71.1
Georgia	59.0	Nebraska	81.2	Utah	92.1
Idaho	83.8	Nevada	87.8	Vermont	71.5
Illinois	81.0	N. Hampshire	74.5	Virginia	63.4
Indiana	79.7	N. Jersey	79.4	Washington	88.9
Iowa	78.1	N. Mexico	70.8	West Virginia	65.0
Kansas	81.2	N. York	88.1	Wisconsin	79.9
Kentucky	49.1	No. Carolina	64.1	Wyoming	85.2
		No. Dakota	70.2		

29. Figures for October 1950 as given by the United States Department of Commerce in *Current Population Reports, Population Characteristics,* U. S. Bureau of Census, Series P-20, No. 34, July 26, 1951, Table 7, p. 11, are shown here in Table 17.

TABLE 17

Percentages of Students in High School

	Boys		Girls	
Age	Public	Private	Public	Private
14 to 17	92.3	7.7	90.9	9.1
18 and 19	97.5	2.5	95.5	4.5

For elementary school enrollment ages 5 to 13 the figures are: public 88.0, private 12.0 (no significant difference between boys and girls). There seems to be no accurate information as to the enrollment between different types of private schools. I have estimated the enrollment in private nonsectarian schools from data given in Tables 53 and 54, U. S. Office of Education, Biennial Survey, Vol. II, 1938–42, Chapter III. For 1939–40 the total private school enrollment was 457,768, about equally distributed between boys and girls; for the Catholic parochial schools the total enrollment is given as 361,000 (of which 157,500 were boys). The difference — 96,768 — gives the figure for boys and girls in private non-Catholic schools; assuming the course of study to be four years and the size of the age group to be 2 million, we have roughly 97,000 out of 8 million, or 1.2 per cent. For boys alone the corresponding estimate would be 1.8 per cent. Allowing for the enrollment in church-connected schools other than Catholic would reduce the figure to less than 1 per cent; on the other hand, the "holding power" (see page 19) of the private boys' boarding school is in all probability considerably higher than that of the church-connected day schools so that for the younger age groups the figure 1.8 is too high, for the older age groups it is too low.

The national average figures such as those given in the preceding paragraph are to some degree misleading because of the wide local variations in the American pattern and because of the fact that there is by no means an equal distribution of different socio-economic groups in the nonsectarian private schools. In some communities few families in the upper income groups will send their children to private schools, in others it will be the exceptional well-to-do parent who patronizes the public school. Some large cities are the spots where enrollment in the private schools is highest, as is shown in Table 18.

TABLE 18

Percentage Distribution of High School Students
(All Ages) between Public and Private Schools *

City	Total Enrollment All Grades	Public	Private
	High Private School Enrollment		
Jersey City, N. J.	50,000	60	40
New Orleans, La.	103,850	61	39
Milwaukee, Wis.	106,769	64	36
Philadelphia, Pa.	319,000	66	34
Cincinnati, Ohio	81,953	69	31
Detroit, Michigan †	314,496	75	25
	Low Private School Enrollment		
Atlanta, · Georgia	52,304	96	4
Ft. Worth, Texas	36,834	96	4
Birmingham, Alabama	47,200	95	5
Oklahoma City, Okla.	37,761	94	6
Dallas, Texas	57,176	92	8
Long Beach, Cal.	43,024	92	8
Houston, Texas	96,500	90	10

* These figures, based on data supplied from the city board of education offices for the fall of 1948, were kindly furnished by Henry H. Hill, President of the George Peabody College for Teachers.

† Figures available from the State Department of Michigan show the same ratio for all grades.

30. For a discussion of the local, state, and federal relations, see Chapter III, note 34, page 154.

Chapter II

1. The figures given in Table 4 are to be regarded as estimates only. For purposes of simplifying the comparison between the five nations an attempt has been made to reduce the statistics available by age groups to the enrollment by years in college or university (first year or freshman, second year or sophomore, and so on). Since all students do not enter universities (or colleges) at one age in a given country and the median age varies from country to country, this method of presentation has the merit of simplicity in showing the general picture. It has been assumed that the maximum percentage of an age group enrolled in a degree-granting institution may be taken as the enrollment of the first-year classes. For the United States the enrollment of the first-year class has been treated as though all freshmen were of one age group and the fairly well-known rate of attrition applied to estimate the enrollment in the subsequent four years. Data by age groups such as that shown for Scotland in Table 12 and for England in Table 19 are not available for the United States. For further discussion of these points, see note 3 to this chapter. The greatest uncertainty in the data for the United States is the lack of information as to how many of the students reported as enrolled in degree-granting institutions are full time. I have assumed that three quarters of the reported enrollments represent full-time students.

The basic information used in making the estimates given in Table 4 was compiled from the following sources.

(1) For England: The data (as shown in Table 19) kindly supplied by the staff of the Ministry of Education for England and Wales (see also Table 7, p. 73, and Table 25, p. 134) are the bases for the calculations.

(2) For Scotland: Data kindly provided by the Scottish Education Department; see Table 12, p. 101. The figures given in Table 4 are an attempt to represent these data assuming a pattern of four full years. As previously noted, the figures for men only are considerably higher. No allowance has been made in these figures for Scots in English universities or vice versa. *The Report of the University Grants Committee for Great Britain on University Development* (1947–51), London (Cmd. 8473), gives the total full-time enrollment for the Scottish universities for 1950–51 as: men, 12,010; women, 3,991; total, 16,001. The size of the age group is approximately 80,000.

(3) (a) For South Australia: Estimates supplied by Mr. V. A. Edgeloe of the University of Adelaide, as shown in Table 20, p. 113.

(b) For New South Wales: Information kindly supplied by Professor C. R. McRae of Sydney University to whom I am particularly indebted for his assistance in my attempts to examine secondary and university education in New South Wales. See Table 7 (p. 73) and Table 8 (p. 74).

(c) For Victoria: Data from the enrollment figures of the University and information supplied by Mr. K. S. Cunningham of the Australian Educational Council.

(4) For New Zealand: From data supplied by the Education Department for 1951 (middle of the academic year). This is shown in Table 21. These

TABLE 19

English Educational Pattern (1951)

Distribution of Boys and Girls between Schools and Other Educational Institutions on a Full-Time and Part-Time Basis in England and Wales (assuming no military service before completion of course)

Percentage of Age Group Enrolled

Age Group	Full Time (Schools)				Full Time (Other Institutions)				Part-Time Education		
	Publicly Maintained	Publicly Aided	Independent		Further Education Establishments	Teacher Training Colleges	Universities	Total Full Time	Day	Evening	Total
			Recognized	Other							
14	88.0	2.5	4.0	4.0	—	—	—	98.5	—	—	—
15	22.0	2.0	4.0	2.0	1.0	—	—	31.0	8.0	34	39
16	9.0	1.5	3.0	1.0	1.5	—	—	16.0	10.5	33	39
17	4.0	0.5	1.5	0.5	1.0	—	—	7.5	9.0	31	37
18	1.5	0.5	0.5	0.5	1.0	2.0	1.5	7.0	5.0	20	22
19	—	—	—	—	0.5	2.0	3.0	5.5	3.0	11	13
20	—	—	—	—	0.5	0.5	3.0	4.0	2.5	8	9
21	—	—	—	—	0.5	—	3.0	3.5	2.0	8	9
22	—	—	—	—	0.5	—	1.5	2.0	2.0	8	9
23	—	—	—	—	—	—	0.5	0.5	—	—	—

TABLE 20

Percentage of Age Group Enrolled, South Australia

| Age Group | University Enrollment | | School of Mines |
	Full Time	Part Time	Part Time
16	0.5	0.5	7
17	1.8	1.8	7
18	3.0	3.0	7
19	3.0	3.0	7

data interpreted in terms of first year being 18 give the figures shown in Table 4.

(5) For the United States: Data given in Circular No. 281, Office of Education, Federal Security Agency (Washington, D. C.) as interpreted with the aid of certain assumptions set forth in detail (note 3, below).

2. The Scottish universities might well claim to be an exception to this generalization. (See Chapter VIII of Alexander Morgan's *Rise and Progress of Scottish Education*, Edinburgh, 1927.) Since 1907 each Scottish university

TABLE 21

Percentage of Age Group Enrolled, New Zealand

Age Group	Teacher College	University Full Time	University Part Time	Technical Part Time
17	1.3	0.8	1.1	11.0
18	3.0	2.8	1.7	9.7
19	2.2	3.1	1.8	6.9
20	0.9	2.8	1.6	5.5
21	—	2.3	1.6	—
22	—	1.4	1.4	—
23	—	1.0	1.3	—

has been allowed to frame its own degree course in the Arts and the study of a combination of subjects rather than specialization in one was introduced at that time. In England as well as Australia and New Zealand, the students enrolled (30 to 40 per cent outside of Oxford and Cambridge) under the Arts faculty of each university are somewhat akin to the American college undergraduates in liberal arts colleges. If one may venture a generalization, however, I would say that there is far less concern with breadth of education and far greater demand for intensive specialization than in the American college. With the exception of Oxford and Cambridge, even in the Arts faculties the students are preparing to ˒se their university training *directly* as, for example, economists or historians or teachers of a language. I have failed to find any appreciable degree of interest in the study of the natural sciences at the university level by students of law or some branch of the social sciences or humanities. Likewise, in both Australia and Great Britain it is freely admitted that boys intending to be scientists, engineers, or doctors will study little history, literature, or the social sciences after the age of 15 or 16 though they may study a foreign language.

An earnest plea for a widening of the outlook of the university graduate has been entered by Sir Walter Moberly, formerly Chairman of the University Grants Committee. "During their years at the university most graduates will have received some vocational training more intensive than of old," he states. "But, over and above this," he declares, "all graduates should have improved their equipment for the major decision they must make; and that is, how to aline themselves on the chief issues which divide our distracted world and by what standard they are to judge them." Sir Walter's *The Universities and Cultural Leadership,* Walker Trust Lectures on Leadership, No. XI (Oxford University Press, 1951).

Government Assistance to Universities in Great Britain, by Dodds, Hacker, and Rogers (memoranda submitted to the Commission on Financing Higher Education, Columbia University Press, New York, 1952) is an interesting summary of many aspects of British university problems as seen through American eyes. "The British Universities in the Post-War Era" by Sir Hector Hetherington, Principal of Glasgow University, reviews the current scene as seen by an experienced head of a British university. (*Proceedings* of the Royal Philosophical Society of Glasgow, Vol. 75, pp. 39–52, 1951). An anonymous discussion of the newer English universities published a few years ago under the title *Redbrick University* contrasts the problems as well as the opportunities of Oxford and Cambridge on the one hand and the newer universities on the other. (Bruce Truscot [pseudonym], *Redbrick University,* London: Faber and Faber Ltd., [1943].) See also D. W. Brogan, "Redbrick Revisited — II" in *Cambridge Journal,* Vol. V, No. 4 (January 1952), pp. 119–120; and Chapter VI by T. R. McConnell of *General Education in Transition* (University of Minnesota Press, 1951).

3. Table 5 (p. 31), attempts to break down the college and university enrollment in terms of (a) types of institutions and programs and (b) the year in college or university (freshman, sophomore, and so on). The only firm data available are total enrollment in colleges and universities — and even these are subject to the uncertainties of full time and part time (see note 1), and the number of students entering for the first time. As to the first, a table taken from *Higher Education for American Democracy,* Vol. VI, Resource Data, Report of the President's Commission on Higher Education (Washington, December 1947), Section IV, Table 20, p. 19, is shown here as Table 22. The last column gives the enrollment in per cent of the age group 18–21 inclusive for both boys and girls.

The figures for the period 1946–1950 are subject to gross misinterpretation because of the influx of veterans. The surest prediction for the immediate future comes from the new enrollments for first-time students in the fall, 1950, which for all institutions, both men and women, were 516,836, including 78,000 veterans, according to Circular No. 281, Federal Security Agency, Office of Education, Table E. Assuming that all these entrants are 18 years of age and taking the size of the age group as 2,143,000 (Department of Commerce, *Current Population Reports,* Series P-20, No. 32), we have 24 per cent (excluding veterans 20 per cent). The corresponding figure broken down by sexes is 319,733 for men and 197,103 for women (Table F in Circular No. 281), which, when calculated in terms of the age group for men, gives the figure of 29 per cent used in Table 5.

Some estimate of the attrition of this 29 per cent during the coming period may be estimated from past performance of colleges and universities in the United States. Approximately half of the students enrolled do not graduate. This would mean that the percentage of an age group who received degrees either at the end of four or five years would be something like 14 per cent. For men only this would be something like 150,000. (This is to be compared with the 329,000 degrees conferred for men only

TABLE 22

Resident Enrollments in Continental United States in Institutions of Higher Education and Relation to College-Age Youth (1900–1947)

Year °	Enrollment	Percentage of College-Age Youth (18–21)
1900	237.592	4.0
1910	355,215	4.8
1920	597,682	8.1
1930	1,100,737	12.2
1932	1,154,117	12.6
1934	1,055,360	11.5
1936	1,208,227	13.0
1938	1,350,905	13.3
1940	1,494,203	15.6
1947	1,354,000 †	15.5

° Twelve months ending June 30.
† This figure does not include 1,000,000 older veterans of World War II.

in 1949–1950, Table F, Circular No. 282, Federal Security Agency, Office of Education (a figure which is far too high because of the veterans). For the last pre-World War II year, 1941–1942, the total number of first degrees conferred was 185,000 (Table A in Circular No. 282). If the ratio of men and women held as now, this would mean there was something like 139,000 men only. A memorandum kindly furnished by the Commissioner of Education, Mr. Earl J. McGrath, estimates the number of Bachelor's and first professional degrees for men only to be awarded in 1955 as 154,000, or about 15 per cent of an age group. I have chosen the conservative figure of 14 per cent for Table 5 as being the total enrollment at the end of four years.

The distribution among the four categories (general four-year course, professional, teachers' training, and junior college) shown in Table 5 is a rough estimate based on the data presented in Table 24, *Higher Education for American Democracy*, Vol. VI, Report of the President's Commission on Higher Education (Washington, 1947). The data there presented are for the year 1947. The proportionate enrollment for junior colleges is perhaps too low and is taken as being 10 per cent of the total first-year group in Table 5 of the text. To the enrollment in teachers' colleges must be added those who are enrolled in colleges and universities for the same purpose, but in Table 5 I have listed my estimate of those in teachers colleges and normal schools only under the heading "teacher training."

The distribution between general four years and professional is obviously arbitrary, and the estimates are accordingly vague. According to the memorandum from the Commissioner of Education, it is expected that there will be something like 60,000 first professional degrees awarded in 1955 of which 22,000 will be in engineering and another 20,000 for subjects in which the first degree after 4 years is often considered the professional degree. In short, two-thirds of the professional degrees are obtained in four years, the remainder as a result of five, six, seven, or eight years' training (for example, law, medicine, dentistry).

Applying these estimates to Table 5 gives a rough estimate of 4 per cent of an age group receiving professional degrees at the end of a four-year course; and assuming a 50 per cent attrition in the teacher training institutions yields a residue of 7 per cent, or 70,000 degrees for four-year general programs for men only.

The reader who is interested in the statistics of university and college enrollments in the United States is referred to the excellent analysis prepared for the Commission on Financing Higher Education (*A Statistical Analysis of the Organization of Higher Education in the United States 1948–49* by Richard H. Ostheimer, Columbia University Press, 1951). It is to be hoped that this type of analysis can be continued, for the data presented for 1948–49 reflect the abnormal veteran enrollment. Tables 1, 2, and 185 analyze the earned degrees for 1948–49 in terms of fields. The difficulties of deciding what fields of study are professional at the undergraduate level are brought out by comparing the figures given in these tables with those in Table 5 (p. 31). Ostheimer classifies undergraduate majors in business or commerce as professional students but those studying economics or home economics as liberal arts. I have counted undergraduate business courses as nonprofessional but included undergraduate work in engineering as professional. The large number taking undergraduate business courses is worthy of note and raises the question of the value of this type of undergraduate work and the standards set for the degree. Ostheimer shows about 34 per cent of degrees as liberal arts, 15 per cent as business, 15 per cent as teachers. If business majors are counted as liberal arts students, the total is about 50 per cent of the total degrees in general agreement with the estimates in Table 5 (Ostheimer's figures are for men and women; my estimates, for men only).

The number of degrees in law represents about 0.8 of an age group as do those degrees in medicine and dentistry combined, and the total of Master's second professional and Doctor's degrees are about the same. Assuming some attrition in the last years of professional study, these figures suggest that perhaps 2 per cent of an age group are enrolled in the fifth year of university study; 1 per cent in the sixth year and considerably less than 1 per cent in the seventh.

All these estimates are made without allowing for the effects of military service. The attempt has been made to compare the pattern of education in the United States with that in other countries, and these figures are reflected in Table 4. For a discussion of the impact of military service, see issue No. 14, Vol. VII, *Higher Education,* a publication of the Office of Education, March 15, 1951.

For the distribution of students in the second and third years, I have merely estimated the rate of shrinkage of the four types of programs listed.

It should be noted that the figures in Table 4, last column, are for boys and girls, and while they reflect the same estimate of distribution between years in professions, they are lower because they are for boys and girls and because they are on a full-time basis.

If one now compares Table 5 with the figures in Table 22, p. 115, it will be evident that the percentage of a four-year age group enrolled in college represents an average figure and is for men and women together and, therefore, lower than the average from Table 5, which would be nearer 20 per cent. This whole note, if nothing else, will impress the reader with the caution with which the statistics about college and university enrollments must be approached.

4. The place of engineering education in the American scene is exceptional in several respects. (Included under engineering in many faculties are architecture and planning.) One is tempted to say that it is the only learned profession which enrolls its student directly on graduation from high school and completes their training at the end of four years. This has always been the case historically. If all other professions in the nineteenth century had followed the example of engineering, there would be no liberal arts college in America today; in other words, we would have the British pattern. Without entering into a long discussion of what is and what is not "a profession" or a "learned profession," two contrary tendencies in the recent development of American "higher" education might be noted. One, the increased number of students who are studying a subject during a four-year course whose mastery is going to equip them for a vocation. The other, the lengthening of engineering courses to five years, and the success of a postgraduate Business School in at least one university. The whole relation of general education to vocational and professional training in the United States appears to be in a chaotic and probably transitory stage.

5. Letter to Joseph C. Cabell in connection with Albemarle Academy (later the University of Virginia), *Early History of the University of Virginia* (Richmond, 1856), p. 37.

6. The data presented in Table 6 are from Table 20, p. 19, Vol. VI, *Higher Education for American Democracy* (see comments in note 3 above); National Education Association *Research Bulletin,* Vol. XXIX, no. 4 (December 1951), Table 16; and U. S. Office of Education, *Biennial Survey* 1942–44, Chapter I, p. 24, Table 18.

A consideration of the increasing importance in the twentieth century of college and university education for women and the history of the growth of coeducation are two of the many subjects relevant to my discussion which I have been forced to omit.

7. The difficulties of obtaining significant statistics about higher education in the United States have already been mentioned (see notes 1 and 3, above).

The difficulties of forecasting the future are even more serious; scholarship provisions, economic conditions, military service, as well as a changing educational philosophy of the nation will all affect the size of our post-high school institutions. For one estimate, see *Higher Education for American Democracy*, Report of the President's Commission on Higher Education (Washington, 1947). For a critical discussion of some of the conclusions, see Seymour E. Harris, *The Market for College Graduates* (Harvard University Press, 1949); and *Education for Democracy? The Debate over the Report of the President's Commission on Higher Education*, edited by Gail Kennedy (Problems in American Civilization), Boston, 1952.

8. S. R. Gardiner, *The Constitutional Documents of the Puritan Revolution* (3rd ed., Oxford, 1906), p. 229; James Haywood and Thomas Wright, *Cambridge University Transactions during the Puritan Controversies of the 16th and 17th Centuries* (London, 1854). See also J. B. Mullinger, *The University of Cambridge*, Vol. III (Cambridge, 1911); C. E. Mallet, *A History of Oxford University* (London, 1924); James B. Conant, "The Advancement of Learning during the Puritan Commonwealth," in *Proceedings of the Massachusetts Historical Society*, Vol. 66, pp. 1–29.

9. For the enrollment of Cambridge, see Mullinger, *The University of Cambridge*, Appendix E, p. 679. For the period 1620–1640 the annual matriculations varied from 350 to 662 (one year of 75 was exceptional); Mallet, *A History of Oxford University*, Vol. II, p. 389, quotes estimates as high as 3,247 students for Oxford in 1651, and this at a time when "prosperity was reviving." Those taking their bachelor's degree numbered 200 annually earlier in the seventeenth century; (p. 141) this would correspond to 400 or 500 matriculations. Mantoux (*The Industrial Revolution in the Eighteenth Century*, London, 1928) quotes estimates of the population of England and Wales in 1650 as five million. This would correspond to from 60,000 to 100,000 in each of the adolescent "age groups" or 30,000 to 50,000 young men (with 155 millions, the United States figure is today 2,000,000, ten years from now it will be 3,000,000). Thus a thousand university entrants might be as many as 2 to 3 per cent of the age group. The figure today is 3.0 per cent (Table 4).

10. See references in note 8, above; see also Dorothy Stimson, *Scientists and Amateurs* (New York, 1948).

11. Samuel Eliot Morison, *Three Centuries of Harvard* (Harvard University Press, 1936), p. 12. "Cost what it might, a real college, in the Oxford and Cambridge sense, they [the founders] would have." And on page 23 Morison writes: "The Charter of 1650 nowhere mentions the training of ministers. The purposes of Harvard College stated in that fundamental document are 'the aduancement of all good literature artes and sciences'; and making 'all other necessary prouisions that may conduce to the education of the English and Indian Youth of this Country in knowledge godlines.'" For a more detailed examination of the relation of early Harvard to Oxford and Cambridge, see *The Founding of Harvard College* by the same author (Harvard University Press, 1935).

12. James Ward of the Harvard Class of 1645 was incorporated B.A. Oxford in 1648 and received the M.A. in the same year; John Collins, A.B. Harvard 1649, who held the Harvard A.M., was incorporated M.A. Cam-

bridge 1654; William Stoughton, Harvard A.B. 1650, was incorporated Oxford B.A. 1652; Leonard Hoar, Harvard A.M. Class of 1650, was incorporated M.A. Cambridge 1654; five others subsequently were received by Oxford or Cambridge. (*Harvard University Quinquennial Catalogue,* 1636–1930, Cambridge, Massachusetts, 1930.)

13. Act of 1701 of the Connecticut Court (Rec. Vol. 4, p. 363) provided for the conferring of degrees "wherein youth may be instructed in the Arts and Sciences." The degree of Bachelor of Arts was conferred on John Hart in 1703.

Previous to the chartering of William and Mary in 1693 there had been negotiations between the Harvard Corporation and the Royal authorities in Massachusetts and London. The revocation of the Massachusetts Bay Charter in 1686 was held to have nullified the Harvard Charter of 1650 and for years attempts were made to obtain a Royal Charter for Harvard. The document known as the Charter of 1692 (which remained in force until disallowed by the King in Council in 1697) contained the statement, "And whereas it is a laudable Custome in Universities whereby Learning has been Encouraged and Advanced to confer Academical Degrees or Titles on those who by their proficiency as to Knowledge in Theology, Law, Physick, Mathematicks or Philosophy have been judged Worthy thereof . . . the President and Fellowes of the said Colledge shall have power from time to time, to grant and admit to Academical Degrees, as in the Universities in England, such as in respect of Learning and Good Manners, they shall find worthy to be promoted thereunto." (Quoted in Morison, *Harvard College in the Seventeenth Century,* Vol. II, p. 491.) Though this Charter was disallowed, there is no evidence that the power to grant degrees was questioned in London. (The Charter of 1650 with no mention of degrees was eventually declared to be in force.)

14. *University of London. The Historical Record Being a Supplement to the Calendar* (London, 1912). The University was chartered by King William IV, November 28, 1836. University College was founded in 1827. "The men who were particularly concerned in bringing University teaching to London were educated neither at Oxford or Cambridge, then the closed preserves of the Anglican Church, nor had they any desire to perpetuate in London the academic traditions which pertain to those ancient seats of learning. Rather they found their inspiration in the philosophy of Jeremy Bentham and a model in the newly-founded University of Berlin." H. A. L. Fisher in Centenary Oration on June 30, 1927, p. 8, in the collection ot Centenary Addresses (London, 1927). University College, however, could not obtain at first a charter to grant degrees (see note 15 below).

15. The chartering of London University was a solution of the problem of whether or not the newly founded University College was to grant degrees. The government decided that at one and the same time they would (a) charter University College as a teaching institution; (b) provide for pupils in this college and in King's College (Anglican) already chartered in 1829 to be examined for degrees to be conferred by London University. The examining body which was to perform all the functions of the Examiners in the Senate House of Cambridge was an entirely separate and independent body to be called the University of London.

The new University can hardly be said to have flourished at the start, for by 1858, after twenty years, only about three hundred students had matriculated and less than one hundred A.B. degrees had been conferred. In the second half of the nineteenth century the exclusive connection with the two affiliated colleges was broken, the base widened, and the numbers increased.

16. A. I. Tillyard, *A History of University Reform* (Cambridge, 1913).

17. H. Hole Bellot, *University College London, 1826–1926* (London, 1929), p. 9.

18. See seventh paragraph of note 26, below, and Chapter III, note 17, p. 135.

19. *Land Grant Colleges and Universities,* Office of Education, Federal Security Agency, Bulletin No. 15, 1951. "The fundamental purpose of the Morrill Act was to insure the development in each state of at least one college adapted to the educational needs of the agricultural and industrial classes. . . . Each state was left to decide whether this new college should be made a part of an already existing institution (commonly the State university) or whether it should be a completely separate institution. . . . From this modest beginning the Federal Government has expanded its contributions to the land-grant colleges and universities. Recognizing the need for research as a basis for developing agriculture, the Congress passed the Hatch Act in 1887 setting up in the land-grant institutions the system of agricultural experiment stations. In 1890 the second Morrill Act was passed supplementing by direct appropriation the income from the land grants for instruction." (P. 2.)

20. Alexis de Tocqueville, *Democracy in America,* abridged edition edited by H. S. Commager (Oxford University Press, 1952), p. 28.

21. *Ibid.,* p. 48.

22. *Ibid.,* pp. 5–6.

23. See the remarks of the New Zealand Minister of Education (Chapter I, p. 20).

24. The Act of 1944 contemplated the raising of the age of compulsory full-time education to 16 and the provision in due course of county colleges for the part-time day education of young people between 16 and 18 who are not in full-time attendance at any school. (*Further Education,* Pamphlet No. 8, Ministry of Education, London, 1947) Sir John Maud has written in his review of "A Century of British Education" (*A Century of British Progress,* Royal Society of Arts, p. 74): "It has been quite impossible to find the building resources or manpower necessary to bring into being the comprehensive pattern of County Colleges envisaged by the 1944 Act. So we must wait for the time when it will be possible to ensure that all young people under 18 who have left school are released from their employment one day a week (or for an equivalent number of weeks in the year) and continue their education by attending County Colleges. Meanwhile, however, industry has shown itself far readier than ever before to release its young employees for education by day as well as by night. And despite the shortage of accommodation for this purpose, probably about half the total number of young people in the county under 18 are already receiving some kind of formal education." For a further discussion of part-time education in British nations see Chapter III, p. 72 and Table 7, p. 73.

25. Address to Conference on Scientific Manpower, American Association for the Advancement of Science, Philadelphia, December 30, 1951.

26. To see ourselves as others see us is always interesting and sometimes highly significant in education as in other matters. Therefore, extracts from a report on American colleges and universities by a group of Englishmen who visited the United States in 1951 are here inserted. (From *Productivity Report on the Universities and Industry*, Report of a Specialist Team, Anglo-American Council on Productivity, London and New York, 1951, pp. 21-23.)

"We found in America a keen and widespread interest in college education and, in comparison with Britain, a more extensive provision of facilities for this education. The principal reason for this public interest seems to be a general urge among all classes to secure the enhanced educational and social status and the improved financial prospects which the possession of a degree is thought to bring. A much larger proportion of young persons embark upon a college education than in Britain.

"The level of attainment reached in American high schools is such that the average entrant to the four-year college course is about two years academically behind his counterpart entering a British university. This has an important bearing upon the standards of college education.

"In America there are both state-owned and privately-owned colleges and universities. In each of these categories there are institutions of high repute, but the range of variation as regards both size and quality is much greater than that which prevails among British universities.

"A high proportion of those who enter American colleges leave before they have completed a degree course. Whereas in Britain this would be regarded as extravagant and educationally undesirable, it is not so regarded in America.

"Except at state institutions where they are frequently negligible, the tuition fees charged by American colleges, both for full-time and for part-time instruction, are high in comparison with fees at British universities. Moreover, scholarships are relatively few in number.

"One of the striking features of American college life is the extent to which students undertake some amount of paid employment during their undergraduate years. While we see some advantage in this practice we take the view that too many extraneous activities of this kind may have educational disadvantages. . . .

"In America, the term 'engineering' has a wide connotation and covers many fields of applied science which in Britain would be called 'technology.'
. . .

"Most engineers in American industry have received their education in degree-granting institutions, there being no considerable alternative source of supply comparable to that which is forthcoming from the technical colleges of Britain. Moreover the view which is sometimes expressed that an engineer is little more than a technical expert in a narrow field is not held in America; rather is it held that for many high executive positions there is no better training than that of the engineer. . . .

". . . We take the view — which we found to be shared by teachers in America who had knowledge and experience of both countries — that as a rule the standard of the American bachelor's degree in science and engineering (B.S.) is at least one year below that of the corresponding British first degree (B.Sc.), that the American student in his master's year will not in general pass beyond the level of the British first degree, but that a doctor's degree (Ph.D.) of one of the better American colleges is comparable to a British doctorate (Ph.D.), though the content of the course will have been somewhat different, having included more advanced instruction and less research. On the other hand, in some American colleges the standard of the doctorate is probably not higher than that of a master's degree at a British university.

"The number of students taking degrees in America greatly exceeds that in Great Britain, even when allowance is made for the different size of population in the two countries. In particular, many more students take a first degree in science and engineering. But when the number of British first degrees (B.Sc.) is compared with the number of American second degrees (M.S.) — which we consider to be the appropriate basis for comparison — the result is not unfavourable to Britain. Moreover, when comparison is made of the output of doctors in America with the British output of masters and doctors, also adjusted on a population basis, it would appear that, although there is an advantage to America in the production of scientists at the higher level, there is an advantage to Britain in respect of engineers at the higher level. . . .

"An important part is played in American industry by men holding a bachelor's degree, particularly in engineering. We believe that these men have no counterpart in Britain. Our graduates have been educated to a higher level and are relatively fewer: the holders of Higher National Certificates are in their narrower technical field advanced as far as, if not farther than, the American graduate, but they have generally obtained their qualifications by part-time study necessarily directed almost entirely towards that technical end."

27. The partial list of external examinations in Table 23 will illustrate the extent to which this feature is of significance in Australian education. (By an external examination is meant an examination set by a committee appointed by the state educational authority or the university. Such examinations test the students' competence with reference to a prepared syllabus.)

Two footnotes to this partial summary of examinations may be in order. First, the number of external examinations has been markedly reduced in the last decade. For example, in New South Wales and South Australia there were formerly external examinations at the end of primary education and examinations for junior technical certificates. In Victoria schools may apply for the right to conduct their own leaving and intermediate examinations and about half the schools have this right. There seems to be a growing tendency to substitute school records (including, of course, internal examinations) for external examinations as criteria for determining the subsequent educational fate of a student.

The second note concerns the difference in average age of the pupils when they enter upon what is called secondary education. In Victoria the age is 12.6, in Queensland 14.5, the other four states 13.2–13.7. In all states entrance to the university depends on passing an examination at the end of the fifth or sixth year of secondary school. In four states this examination is the School Leaving Certificate Examination; in two others there is a special University matriculation examination taken a year after the School Leaving Certificate Examination.

28. A few words of explanation about examinations at this point may be helpful, for Americans are so little used to the British examination system that it is difficult to refer to it in a meaningful way. Since early in the nineteenth century, when the University of London came into existence, the British have thought of universities as organizations not only for teaching,

TABLE 23

External Examinations Used in Various States in Australia

Average Age of Student	External Examination	States using this type of examination
11.7	High School Entrance	Victoria
12.8	High School Entrance Secondary School Scholarship	Western Australia
13.4	High School Entrance	Queensland
14.4	Proficiency Certificate Junior Technical Certificate	Victoria, South Australia
15.0–15.3	Intermediate Certificate or Junior Certificate	New South Wales (internal), Victoria, Queensland, South Australia, Western Australia
16–16.5	Leaving Certificate (Also matriculation South Australia)	Victoria, South Australia, New South Wales (16.9)
16–17	Leaving Honors Certificate or Matriculation (set by University)	New South Wales, Victoria, Queensland, South Australia, Western Australia

but also for examining. The standards of degrees were assured throughout the Empire (later the Commonwealth) by having a body of eminent professors responsible for setting the examinations and grading them. The amount of time and labor of highly competent scholars that is thus consumed throughout the British Commonwealth is amazing to an American. "University colleges" in the British sense are teaching institutions which prepare students to "sit" for university examinations but the staff is not empowered to decide by examination or otherwise who shall be granted degrees.

The University of London is, for example, primarily an examining and degree-granting institution; it enrolls no students, teaches no students. The students are enrolled and taught by a number of university colleges and other institutions in and around London (and a few at a distance); each of these has its own standards of admission and instruction. These teaching organizations cannot grant degrees; the degrees are granted by the University of London.

By a series of complicated academic devices the controlling body of the University of London (the Senate) sees to it that the professors of the University (who are members of the professorial staff of the various teaching colleges) maintain high standards for the various degrees. The newer universities in England (for example, Manchester, Bristol, and Birmingham) are at one and the same time university colleges and universities; that is, they are both teaching and examining institutions. So too are the Australian universities. The University of New Zealand, on the other hand, is like London University, solely an examining and degree-granting institution. The four constituent university colleges are the University of Otago at Dunedin, Canterbury University College at Christchurch, Victoria University College at Wellington, and Auckland University College at Auckland.

A British university that is both a teaching and examining institution is clearly under an obligation to enroll only those who stand a reasonable chance of passing the examination required for the degree in question. The professors of the university, through academic committees, determine the standards for the degree. They thus determine *as part of this standardizing process* the requirements for admission to the university course of study leading to each degree. This means, of course, that they determine to a considerable extent the secondary school curriculum for those who have any intention of entering a university. It is not too much to say that the standards of the degree require a fairly rigidly prescribed course of study starting at age 13. It is perfectly logical, therefore, for the university to participate in testing the students in the schools from time to time to see if, at every stage of the journey, progress has been satisfactory. Thus, in Australia the idea of "external" examinations has been accepted for a long time. These are examinations set by some agency external to the secondary school; the agency is an arm of the state but in practice always includes some university people. External examinations obviously require a prescribed course of study and the syllabus for each subject is prepared by committees responsible to the ministry of education, and again the influence of university men is far from negligible. Clearly the examination required for admission to the university (the matriculation examination) is an external examination and both its contents (the syllabus) and its administration are matters solely for university determination.

29. A state in the United States could likewise coördinate its education by means of examinations. Few have tried to do so, but those readers who are familiar with education in New York State will be less surprised than others at the idea of a State supervised set of school examinations. For the so-called "Regents Examinations" of high school students in New York State long filled somewhat the same function as the Leaving Certificate Examinations in Australia. Very great changes have been made in these examinations in recent years. Like the College Board Entrance Examinations (used by many Eastern colleges) the shift has been from factual examinations closely related to syllabi to the objective type of test which aims to measure "scholastic aptitude" rather than specific knowledge.

The following quotations from a bulletin (June 1, 1950) issued by Harry V. Gilson, Associate Commissioner, to the Superintendents and Principals of Secondary Schools of New York State may be of interest.

"The state examinations program was established by the Board of Regents in 1864 with the introduction of a system of preliminary examinations. These examinations were based principally on the curriculum of the seventh and eighth years of the traditional elementary school. They were first used as a basis for admitting and classifying pupils as high school pupils and for state-aid purposes. The initial success of the preliminary examinations in the standardization of instruction led to the introduction of a system of academic or high school examinations in 1878. On the recommendation of secondary school and college authorities these examinations were designed to serve as a basis for high school graduation and admission to college. In these early years the academies and high schools were primarily college preparatory in function and served a very small and scholastically screened pupil population.

"Indeed there were fewer than 10,000 fully qualified academic pupils enrolled in the private and public high schools of the State in 1878. There were fewer than 100,000 pupils enrolled in all high schools in 1900. By 1925 the total enrolment had increased rapidly to approximately 335,000 pupils. Almost double this enrolment is found in our public and private high schools in the present school year 1949–50. . . . No longer primarily college preparatory in function, our high schools today are concerned with the general education of all our youth and with the preparation of boys and girls as individuals for the kind of social, economic and scientific world in which they must live. . . .

". . . During the past two years the State Examinations Board has carefully studied the place and function of Regents examinations in relation to a broad program of testing services as they affect the total educational program in the schools of the State."

There follows a series of seven changes, the first six of which still further reduce the function of the Regents Examinations as "external examinations" setting standards in subject matter. The seventh is as follows:

"Regents examinations are recommended to the schools for general supervisory purposes and as partial measures of achievement for pupils of average and above average ability who pursue courses of study within a curriculum framework upon which Regents examinations are based."

The examinations, if properly used, today will serve as part of the school testing and guidance program. They are not adequate and are not intended to be used for measuring the accomplishment of all high school pupils. The local schools are now obligated to develop internal examinations and other means of evaluating the learning of pupils who may not properly be served by Regents examinations.

30. See Chapter I, note 22, p. 105. An external examination is still given in New Zealand at age 16+ but since four out of some thirty subjects may be offered in addition to English a wide latitude is given the school. When the University changed its entrance procedures, a matriculation examination was no longer required for boys and girls who are accredited by the school. The examination is used for those who are not accredited by the school or for those from the schools which do not have the right to accredit.

31. Information kindly supplied by officers of the Department of Education. For matriculation in the University of Sydney one must pass in one

examination period at least five subjects of which one must be English and the other four subjects must be chosen from certain groupings corresponding to certain rules. These would indicate that such orthodox combinations as the following were possible and I should judge frequent: English, French, Latin, Algebra and Geometry; English, French, Algebra and Geometry, Physics; English, Algebra and Geometry, Physics, Chemistry. Less orthodox combinations appear possible and their occurrence might indicate why the Sydney professors I met refused to agree that all their students came to them with a thorough knowledge of mathematics and a foreign language: for example, English, Modern History, Algebra, Theory and Practice of Music, Geography. In order to enter the University of Adelaide, the candidate must pass an examination in at least one foreign language, Algebra and Geometry. But the influence of the university extends beyond these prescriptions. Students who wish to study a physical science know they must take physics and chemistry in school if they are to succeed in the university.

The interplay between the matriculation requirements of the university in each state and the curricula of the schools is curious. The private schools are in theory relatively free to experiment with their curricula and are bound only by the matriculation requirements of the university; I found the private school masters, therefore, more than once in the vanguard of those pressing for a liberalization of the university requirements. The officers of the Department of Education (who have no control over the university) are interested in liberalizing the curriculum to the degree that they wish experimentation within their system. This seems to have been the case particularly in New South Wales. Yet in Sydney the most famous high school has a highly orthodox curriculum (one might almost say an 1870 curriculum!). Therefore, the liberalization of the matriculation requirements of a university may have no effect on the actual content of the course of many students.

32. *General Education in Transition* (The University of Minnesota Press, 1951), Chapter VI, p. 91.

33. Foreword to *General Education in Science* (Harvard University Press, 1952).

34. *Higher Education for American Democracy*, Report of the President's Commission on Higher Education (Washington, 1947). See note 7, above, p. 117.

Chapter III

1. The figures in Table 24 for the live births in recent years indicate that fifteen years from now there will be 65 per cent more youths of college age than at the present time.

2. The curricula of the Australian schools are discussed in note 19 to Chapter I, p. 103; the program of New Zealand schools in note 24 to Chapter I, p. 106. See also Chapter II, pp. 49–51, and notes 27 and 31, pp. 122 and 125.

3. *Education for All American Youth, A Further Look,* Educational

Policies Commission of the National Education Association and the American Association of School Administrators (Washington, D. C., 1952, pp. 224–229.) The authors describe a continuous course using two or more hours daily throughout grades ten to fourteen planned to help *all* students grow in competence as citizens of the community and the nation. Such a course in "Common Learnings" was "planned specifically to meet the educational needs of youth in the fields of citizenship, economics, family living, appreciation of literature and the arts, and the use of the English language" (p. 228).

4. Throughout the discussion of a future program for colleges, I have made what I am afraid is a most unrealistic assumption, namely, that the

TABLE 24

Approximate Number of Annual Births in the United States *

1930	2,200,000
1935	2,155,000
1940	2,360,000
1945	2,735,000
1950	3,548,000

* Figures for the years 1930–1945 obtained from *Statistical Abstract of the United States,* 1951; figure for the year 1950 obtained from *Monthly Vital Statistics Bulletin,* Federal Security Agency.

United States will not have to keep a large number of men under arms. Actually, we shall soon be faced with the prospect of having to draft essentially all our able-bodied youth for two years of military service. Even in 1952 a considerable portion of young men of college age are facing the prospect of several years of service either as officers or enlisted men. The arguments for shortening the formal period of education are reinforced by the existence of an international situation which may well require two years of service of all young men for another ten or twenty years. I am firmly of the opinion that this service should be performed immediately after the completion of the high school course. For those going on to professional study, time could be saved by using the summers for college or university work. To offset the loss in summer earnings so important for many young Americans, Federal funds are now available to the returning soldier or sailor under the new G.I. Bill. How to accommodate scientists, engineers, doctors, and dentists into such a program is a question that leads one into a highly controversial area.

5. *Education for All American Youth, A Further Look* (see note 3, above). Chapter I (pp. 7–8) points out how recent is the development of secondary education for *all* American youth. "Not until after the first world war was there widespread official recognition of a public secondary school substantially independent of the college, with objectives of its own and responsibilities to American youth of all sorts . . . Today, we stand somewhere midway between the traditional secondary education designed for only a small fraction of youthful society and the education for all youth

which is now so imperatively necessary to individual, community, and national welfare . . .

"When we say that we are now approximately midway in the development of education for all youth, we do not mean midway in time, but midway in result . . ."

6. See also Chapter I, note 7, page 93, and Chapter II, page 51, for a discussion of the curricula in English schools.

For an interesting discussion of the movement in England for the introduction of the comprehensive school, see President H. W. Dodds' "Memorandum on Government Grants in Aid to Universities in Great Britain," *Government Assistance to Universities in Great Britain* (Columbia University Press, 1952), pp. 124–133. He writes in part as follows:

"However, egalitarian reform pressures do not end with the establishment of secondary schools for all, and the tripartite system is not proving radical enough for Left Wing socialists. To the goal of secondary education for all is added a demand in more radical circles that there shall be no distinctions in social prestige among the three types. So one hears of the precautions necessary to assure 'parity of esteem' for the three elements of the tripartite curriculum. The means proposed to guarantee parity of esteem are the so-called 'comprehensive' schools. The essence of the comprehensive school idea is that it will accommodate in one school all the secondary education needs of a given geographical area. By this means it is expected that the social stratification, which the tripartite system tends to preserve, will be prevented. Without parity of esteem, says Labour, there can be no true equality of opportunity in education. . . .

"Unfortunately, in the effort to promote esteem for the modern school curriculum and popular acceptance of the comprehensive school idea, it has seemed necessary for its advocates to depress esteem for the grammar school and to advocate policies which seriously endanger its excellence. . . .

"The pedagogical arguments for and against the comprehensive school are many, but there is no need to review them in detail. Its critics who are familiar with our system see in it but a copy of 'American mass education' which neglects proper attention to the individual scholar. In concentrating attention upon the 'common child,' it is charged, the sound education of the uncommon child will go by the board. In talks with representatives of the Labour Party, I raised various questions, such as would immediately occur to one reasonably familiar with the points of the strength and weaknesses of the American high school system, and was convinced that the 'parity of esteem' ideal embodies familiar dangers, even probabilities, which its advocates tend to gloss over."

7. I have suggested that too much of our educational planning is done on the assumption that there are no economic, cultural, and religious cleavages in American society. Yet one is loath to emphasize these cleavages in public discussion because the very process of delineating the social strata tends to increase the degree of stratification. Yet for those who like myself are convinced that American society can even today remain relatively fluid, it is important both to work for a greater degree of social mobility and to recognize frankly the social strata in existence in various communities. In my *Education in a Divided World* (Harvard University Press, 1948, Chapter

III) and the Sachs Lectures at Columbia University on "Public Education and the Structure of American Society" (*Teachers College Record*, XLVII (1945), 145–194) I have discussed these matters at some length.

For a discussion of some eductional problems by professional sociologists, the reader may be referred to *Who Shall Be Educated?* by Warner, Havighurst and Loeb (Harper Bros., New York, 1944) and "The Supply and Identification of High Level Talent" by R. J. Havighurst in the 1951 *Proceedings of Invitational Conference on Testing Problems*, Educational Testing Service (Princeton, New Jersey). In this last article the author emphasizes the great importance of the motivational factor in determining the supply of "high ability" people who go to college. He concludes that "apparently the motivation for college training is much greater among the top 2 per cent of the population than it is among the top 20 per cent . . . even in the top 2 per cent there may be as many as a third . . . who do not seek college-level training . . . Yet it is probably true that, due to our system of universal education, to a relatively high degree of economic opportunity, and to our culture which rewards or at least tolerates a wide variety of talents, our society probably has the greatest amount of visible and developed talent that any human society has had."

8. *Education of the Gifted*, Educational Policies Commission (Washington, 1950). In the Foreword it is stated that "The educational needs of individuals who have superior intellectual capacity and of those who possess special talents in high degree differ in some important respects from the needs of other individuals. To capitalize the rich resources of human talent which gifted children and youth possess, the schools and colleges must give special attention to the education of their gifted students. This policy, clearly stated in 'Education for *All* American Youth' and 'Education for All American Children,' needs further emphasis and elaboration.

"Acquaintance with present educational practices has convinced the Commission that the gifted members of the total school population constitute a minority which is too largely neglected. Part of the neglect stems from attitudes widely held among the American people, attitudes which tend to obscure the great social need for able and educated leaders and to withhold needed funds for making adequate educational opportunities available to all gifted youth. Part of the neglect results from the circumstance that inadequate buildings and equipment and an insufficient supply of teachers prevent schools and colleges from doing as much as they would like to do in differentiating instruction. But the education of gifted children and youth also suffers from a too frequent failure on the part of teachers and administrators to give enough attention to the problems of identifying the gifted, counseling them, and making special provisions for their education. Although many excellent educational programs designed to meet the special needs of the gifted are in operation, such programs could doubtless benefit from further improvement and from a broader base of lay and professional understanding as to their purpose and importance.

. . . We specifically wish to re-state our conviction that *all* children and youth, including the gifted, should devote a substantial portion of their school time to 'common studies' designed to serve the common needs of all — studies that will improve proficiency in the use of language and numbers, civic and economic competence, family relationships, aesthetic appreciation, health and physical education, and an understanding of the basic principles and social implications of science. Beyond this basic program for all, the earlier reports also recommended that gifted students (and each other special category of students) should have additional educational experiences appropriate to their special needs. . . .

" . . . Moreover, although this statement must necessarily emphasize the distinguishing needs and characteristics of the gifted, the apparent emphasis on differences should not be taken as a sign of indifference to the large areas of common needs and characteristics which the gifted share with all their fellows. . . ."

Specifically this document recommends for the "highly gifted" (1 per cent of the population) the following secondary school program:

"(1) A *foreign language;* studied for a long enough time and with sufficient intensity to achieve, at least, reading mastery.

"(2) Advanced *mathematics;* certainly through advanced algebra, probably through trigonometry, possibly through calculus.

"(3) Additional study of the *social studies,* with emphasis on history, beyond the amount taken by the typical high-school student.

"It has been said that 'nearly every highly gifted student' should follow the program outlined above. There are two exceptions. (1) The youth who is highly gifted in music or art as well as in general intelligence may safely omit advanced mathematics but not social studies or foreign language. (2) The highly gifted youth who suffers from physical disability or from social or emotional maladjustment in adolescence to the extent that intensive academic work for him in high school may be either impossible or undesirable should have his high-school program modified accordingly.

"With these exceptions, we recommend the above program for *all* highly gifted youth. . . .

"Many *moderately* gifted students could also profit from more social studies, advanced mathematics, and foreign language in high school; but in their case the need is neither so clear nor so compelling as it is in the case of the highly gifted.

"While we recommend these academic studies for gifted students, we also insist that this type of program should *not* be required of the majority of young persons enrolled in secondary schools. Attempts to impose such a program on students who have little need or aptitude for it still exist in many schools and sometimes gain support from parents and others who fail to recognize the realities of individual differences in relation to higher education and life work. Educators need to face candidly the educational and vocational implications of individual differences in mental ability and to help parents and schoolboard members, as well as youth, to understand these implications.

"The principles of curriculum differentiation for gifted students that have here been recommended to govern the choice of elective courses in high school also apply to some extent to the choices that have to be made during the undergraduate years of higher education. At this level, of course, preparation for post-graduate specialization and lifetime career will have chief influence on the choice of elective courses. The tendency of some gifted college students to select their courses within a narrow range and so move rapidly into advanced work of a highly specialized nature should be discouraged. A broad base of general education on the college level should be a required part of the program for all gifted students."

9. As a matter of statistics the high school graduate does better than the private school boy in Harvard College though he may have considerable difficulty the first year. Thus, of those graduating *Magna cum Laude* or *Summa cum Laude* in 1951 and 1952, two thirds were from public schools though the classes as a whole were about 50 per cent composed of public school graduates. However, these statistics are to some degree misleading, for only the top quarter of the class of many high schools apply for admission to Harvard whereas all the graduates of a private preparatory school are potential college students. As I have pointed out in reviewing education in Australia and New Zealand, the standards set by a college or university for admission determine to a considerable extent the nature of a preparatory school course. In the United States the movement in the last twenty years has been to emphasize scholastic ability or aptitude rather than achievement. The new-type tests (objective tests) now prepared by the Educational Testing Service for the College Entrance Examination Board provide information about a candidate for admission that enables one to predict fairly accurately the student's subsequent academic work in college.

The use of intelligence tests of various sorts, including the verbal and mathematical parts of the Scholastic Aptitude Tests for selecting students for schools or colleges, has been challenged both by conservative educators and by those concerned with the education of low-income groups. That they are still imperfect instruments everyone would concede. Furthermore, they must be used intelligently. Nevertheless, a combination of such tests (frequently given) and an accumulative school record provides far more reliable information for guidance than the old-fashioned external examinations based on the syllabus of the usual academic disciplines.

Guidance is the keystone of the arch of public education; every effort to improve the guidance services in our schools should be encouraged and the improvement of objective tests of various types is of the greatest importance. *Education in a Divided World*, pp. 136–143; *Education for All American Youth*, pp. 49–52, 189–190; B. L. Johnson, "General Education in Action," American Council on Education (Washington, D. C., 1952), Chapter IV, pp. 54–77.

10. Those who adhere to the belief in the value of a classical curriculum will rarely, if ever, find a public school that is to their minds satisfactory. Neither will those who demand that the student entering college should have a knowledge of two foreign languages as well as a good grounding in mathematics. One of the difficulties of providing adequately for the gifted boy or girl is that schoolmasters and professors today hold such a variety of views as to what is a "good" secondary school course. For my part, if a considerable fraction of the youth with an I.Q. of 110 and over were to finish high school with a reading knowledge of *one* foreign language, some ability to write English, and a well-developed skill in handling high school mathematics, we should be well advanced on the road to an American

educational millennium (I am assuming in addition some acquaintance with English literature, social studies, and the natural sciences). For the very gifted boy or girl, more mathematics or an additional language might well be provided. (See note 8, above.)

11. *Education for* All *American Youth, A Further Look* recommends the following arrangement for a city school (page 231). Elementary education grades 1–6 (ages 6–11), preceded by kindergarten and nursery school; grades 7–9, Lower Secondary School (Junior High School); grades 10–12, Middle Secondary School (Senior High School); grades 13 and 14, Advanced Secondary School (Community College with roads to liberal arts colleges, technical schools, and professional schools starting from the end of grades 12, 13, and 14. (For the curriculum, see p. 233.)

12. The Australian Commonwealth Scholarships have recently been established (1950) by the National Government for students attending the universities in Australia which are *state* universities. (The Commonwealth Government is not directly concerned with education at any level except for the support of the National University in the capital, Canberra.) The full impact of the plan has not yet been felt. Three thousand scholarships a year are to be provided. The present enrollment of the eight universities (one in each state plus the National University and the New South Wales University of Technology in Sydney) is about the equivalent of 25,000 students. Therefore, if the total enrollment does not go up in four years' time, something like four times three thousand, or twelve thousand students, or half the student body would be thus supported. However, many people believe that the enrollment will double in this period and likewise the social composition of the student body will be markedly affected. State scholarships continue to be available also, so as many as 75 per cent of the students in some universities may be receiving some public money.

The American reader must remember that the mere location of seven of the eight universities in the metropolitan area of each state already offers excellent educational facilities for many full-time and part-time students at low cost. (All the universities, except that of Western Australia located in Perth, charge fees, but these are not unduly heavy.) The Commonwealth Scholarships will take care of all fees and those students "who wish to undertake approved full-time courses on a full-time basis may also apply for living allowances, which will be payable subject to a means test. The maximum living allowance will be £130 per annum in the case of a student living with his parents and £195 per annum in the case of a student living away from his parents. These maximum living allowances [1951] are payable when the adjusted family income of the student and his parents does not exceed £400." (The adjusted family income is the taxable income corrected for allowances for dependent children.) (Pamphlet of Universities Commission, Commonwealth of Australia, *Details of the 3,000 Scholarships,* 1951, p. 5.)

Twelve thousand scholarships for essentially professional training (see page 30) for a nation of the size of Australia is equivalent to about two hundred thousand scholarships (but all of very high standards!) in the United States for students in law, medicine, engineering, and specialized courses in science, economics, linguistics, history. The cost of the Australian plan is expected to be around a million pounds (or was so estimated at 1951 prices) or about 0.03 per cent of the national income; this would appear to be equivalent to an expenditure of about $100,000,000 a year by the Federal Government in the United States.

The Australian scholarships are awarded "entirely on merit on the results of public examinations qualifying students for matriculation and no regard will be paid to the means of a student's parents" (*Details of the 3,000 Scholarships*, p. 6). The contrast between this procedure and that used for determining educational benefits under the G.I. Bill for World War II veterans need hardly be underlined.

13. "Utilization of the Experience of Work in the Learning Process," in 1948 *Yearbook*, American Association of School Administrators, (Washington, D. C., 1949), pp. 164–167.

Of the schools reporting work experience programs, more than half reported that these programs had been started since 1940. Of the 140 schools surveyed for 1946–1947 programs in each of the grades from 7 through 11, the median per cent of pupils participating was 11 per cent of the enrollment or less. In grade 12 the median per cent of pupils in the programs was 13.7 per cent; but in 16 of the 111 schools having programs in the twelfth grade, 40 per cent or more of the pupils were involved. (Stuart Anderson, "High School Work Experience Programs in Action," *School Board Journal*, August 1951.) For other articles dealing with the recent expansion of work experience programs, see also: Sampson and Jacobson, "Controversial Issues Involved in Work Experience Programs," in *Bulletin of the National Association of Secondary School Principals* (January 1950), p. 215; M. M. Rudinger, "The High-School Vocational Counselor Uses the Community," in *ibid.* (May 1950), p. 66; L. W. Miller, "Education for Work," Chapter III of *Review of Educational Research*, 1950.

14. A condensed statement of the principles set forth in *Education for All American Youth, A Further Look*, pp. 346–347.

15. The data given in Table 7 were kindly supplied by the staff of the Ministry of Education. The corresponding figures for girls (Table 25) may be of interest. A comparison with those given for boys in Table 7 will make evident the fact that while there is little difference between the sexes as far as full-time education is concerned, except for the universities, the part-time enrollment is appreciably less in the case of girls.

16. Sydney is not the only locality in New South Wales where part-time technical education is available. Other much smaller communities offer technical part-time instruction: Newcastle and Broken Hill for example. For those who live in the rural areas and small towns, however, educational opportunity apart from extensive correspondence courses would seem to consist of attendance at the state school followed by transfer of domicile to Sydney for full- or part-time university work (or Teachers' College, or part-time technical education).

The figures for South Australia and Victoria similar to those in Tables 8 and 9 show a similar high proportion of the age groups 15 to 18 pursuing some type of education, but only a small percentage enrolled for full-time work.

TABLE 25

Distribution of Girls in England and Wales in Educational Establishments Full Time and Part Time (January 1951) *

Percentage of Age Group (Female) Enrolled

Age Group	Full Time (Schools)				Full Time (Other Institutions)				Part-Time Education		
	Publicly Maintained	Publicly Aided	Independent		Further Education Establishments	Teacher Training Colleges	Universities	Total Full Time	Day	Evening	Total
			Recognized	Other							
14	87.5	2.5	4.0	4.0	—	—	—	98.0	—	—	—
15	21.5	2.0	3.5	2.0	1.5	—	—	30.5	6.0	33	37
16	9.0	1.0	2.5	1.0	1.5	—	—	15.0	6.0	29	33
17	4.0	0.5	1.0	0.5	1.0	—	—	7.0	4.0	27	30
18	1.0	—	0.5	—	1.0	2.5	1.0	6.0	1.5	18	19
19	—	—	—	—	0.5	3.0	1.5	5.0	1.0	12	13
20	—	—	—	—	0.5	1.0	1.5	3.0	1.0	7	8
21	—	—	—	—	0.5	—	1.5	2.5	1.0	7	8
22	—	—	—	—	—	—	0.5	0.5	1.0	7	8

* Excludes nursing; 18 yrs., 3.0 per cent; 19 yrs., 4.5 per cent; 20 yrs., 4.0 per cent; 21 yrs., 1.0 per cent.

17. In Australia in recent years summer work for university students has become more common and part-time employment for a student registered full time in a university less rare. The trend in the British nations, including England, seems to be in the direction of the American practice. Nevertheless, as of today the contrast between American and British practice is striking. One must also recognize the existence in America of several institutions in which full-time education alternates with full-time work experience. Antioch College has had this arrangement for a number of years with students in all programs, and several engineering schools have followed a similar pattern. (See also notes 13 and 14, above.)

18. The substance of this section was originally presented as the last half of the third Page-Barbour Lecture at the University of Virginia on February 14, 1952; in a slightly different form and with the addition of a few paragraphs from the first lecture (about Australia), it was read at a meeting of the American Association of School Administrators in Mechanics Hall, Boston, Massachusetts, on April 7, 1952. The text was subsequently printed in the Harvard *Alumni Bulletin* for April 19, 1952; and also in the *Saturday Review* for May 3, 1952, together with replies by Archbishop Cushing and the headmaster of Lawrenceville, Mr. A. V. Heely. The first reports of my speech in the press were not in all respects accurate and failed to distinguish between alarm at any considerable further expansion of private schools and a desire to see private schools eliminated. Another source of confusion was the fact that the word "school" has now come to mean college or university to many Americans and my failure to insert the adjective "secondary" in every case seems to have led some readers astray. The section has now been written with a view to meeting some of the objections raised by my correspondents. In this connection the following letter which I wrote to a teacher in a private boarding school may be of interest:

"Dear Mr. ———:

"I am disturbed that as an instructor at an independent undenominational secondary school you feel that my speech was 'an indictment of private secondary education.' Obviously I have failed to make myself clear.

"I should be the first to admit that certain private secondary schools have played an important role in this nation for several generations. I believe they will continue to do so for years to come. While I regard the comprehensive tax-supported high school as the ideal school for an American community, there are many cities and towns where such schools are lacking or, alas, totally inadequate. This is particularly true in regard to their ability to prepare gifted children for college and university work. They should be made better in this respect, and this was one of the two main points in my address to the School Administrators. If in a given community the choice were between improving the comprehensive high school and founding a private school, I would heartily endorse the former course. Nevertheless, since tolerance of diversity is a cardinal principle of our free society, I would never think of supporting legislation which would be a block to the establishment of a proposed new private school. On the other hand, I should be opposed to using tax money directly or indirectly to help such a school.

"Within limits, competition between public high schools and private schools is of benefit to our society. I say 'within limits' for I should regard it as most unfortunate if in a community now served by a satisfactory comprehensive high school enrolling essentially all the students of secondary school age, this school should be replaced by a group of private schools, each drawing students from families differentiated on religious or economic lines.

"That many people would disagree with me on this last point I am well aware. And I think every teacher in a private school ought to think through clearly where he or she stands on this great issue now facing American education. There can be no question but that churchmen in more than one denomination are anxious to expand the number and scope of the church schools. Some of these people desire to use tax money for this purpose, either directly or indirectly. In other words, they would change what has become the accepted American pattern of secondary education into one resembling the English pattern in which different religious schools receive public funds. I feel as strongly as I can that to change the American picture by destroying or crippling our unique product — the comprehensive public high school — would be to undermine our democracy. If you agree with me on this point, you will be as much opposed as I am to those critics of the public schools who try to discredit them by calling them 'Godless' or erroneously describing them as 'state schools.' Everyone is well aware that diversity in public education in the United States results from the fact that the doctrine of local responsibility for our tax-supported schools is part of our basic philosophy. Our public schools are not state controlled but the responsibility of local groups.

"Teachers in church schools and I would, of course, have to agree to disagree strongly on many points. Proponents of expansion of private schools and I would disagree. But because one type of institution should not be expanded is no reason for condemning it. For example, I think our four-year colleges should not be expanded in number or scope, but I hardly need say I think their continuance is of great importance. In this connection I might point out that at the college level there is no equivalent of a comprehensive public school. Even a state-supported university accommodates no more than a small fraction of the youth of college age. Both public and private colleges face the same problem in keeping the road to their institutions open for young men and women from all income groups.

"As one teacher to another, I venture to conclude by suggesting that whether the school or college that any one of us labors in is ideally suited to our society will always remain a debatable point. But that each teacher has a paramount duty to do the best he can for his students we can both agree, and applaud the excellent work of the members of our profession wherever it is performed.

"Sincerely yours,"

19. Chapter 9 of *Education for* All *American Youth: A Further Look* (1952 edition) describes a state system of education which the authors believe to be best suited for the United States in the years ahead. Under the head-

ing "The State Department and the Local School Districts," the following paragraph occurs (p. 339):

"The superintendent of public instruction and other members of the staff of the state department of education are thoroughly committed to the principle that schools should be controlled chiefly by local governing boards and their chief executive officers and staffs with only the necessary minimum of control by state officials. The department staff believes that, if the community is relieved of responsibility for the operation of its schools, the schools will sooner or later lose touch with the life of the community."

Later (on p. 344) it is stated that "The law gives the state board of education authority to determine, in broad outline, the scope of the educational program to be provided in local communities. The board has consistently used its authority to define only the minimum essentials of the curriculum. Every district enjoys wide latitude to exceed the prescribed minimum, to adapt the curriculum to its local conditions, and to experiment with new fields and methods of instruction."

The actual situation in many of the forty-eight states of the Union is that the chief educational authority of the state plays a far less important role than that contemplated by the authors of *Education for All American Youth*. It was the absence of strong state leadership in the 1930's that made possible the dangerous intrusion of a Federal agency into the field of education. Many will have forgotten the rapid growth of a system of Federal schools for special purposes during the depression days. At that time there was a real threat to local control by the use of Federal money for the *direct* support of schools. The nature of the threat and ways of meeting it were analyzed by the Educational Policies Commission in 1941 in a pamphlet entitled *The Civilian Conservation Corps, the National Youth Administration and the Public Schools*.

Hostile critics of the public schools in the United States sometimes refer to them as "state schools." This is hardly an accurate use of words. The public schools of each of the Australian states are state schools (Chapter I, page 26). It is a matter of importance to see that the free schools in America do not become state schools but continue as local schools. At the same time, in some states far more effective leadership is required by state authorities to insure minimum standards and adequate legislation in support of the local schools and community colleges. New York State and the State of Washington are famous for their strong state departments of education, but it would be erroneous to designate the public schools even in these states as "state schools." (For a description of the situation in various states see *The 48 State School Systems*, Council of State Governments, Chicago, 1948.)

A few facts may be of interest. In two states — New Jersey and Connecticut — the local school superintendents are appointed either by the State Commissioner or the State Board. I hazard the opinion that this is not a practice to be emulated as it would seem to go contrary to the doctrine of local control. In Maryland the superintendents appointed by the local boards must have the approval of the State Superintendent. The minimum educational requirements for teachers is determined in most states by state law, but the appointment of teachers is by the local boards. (The contrast with the state schools in Australia is here marked, for the training and employment of teachers is a function of the central educational authority in each Australian state.) State adoption of textbooks is a practice that from my point of view has little to commend it. Only nine states have "single adoption lists" for their elementary schools. There is only one state — Oregon — which has a single adoption list for its secondary schools. In a number of states the state authorities must approve a textbook adopted by a local board but in general there seems to be little control by a central authority of books used in secondary schools.

20. See Chapter I, note 29, page 109 for the wide variation in the private school enrollment in some cities in the United States. That the trend is in the direction of a greater percentage of adolescents attending private schools is evident from the figures in Table 26.

TABLE 26

Percentage of Children in School (All Grades) Enrolled in Private Schools (Including Church Schools)

Year	City of Detroit	State of Michigan	State of Massachusetts	Cities of Massachusetts
1930	23.3	13.3	—	—
1938	—	—	24.8	32.0
1940	21.5	13.0	—	—
1950	25.1	15.5	31.8	44.1
1951	25.4	16.0	—	—

The data for Detroit and Michigan were supplied by the Department of Public Instruction, Lansing, Michigan; those for Massachusetts are from the Annual Reports of the Massachusetts Department of Education.

21. Table 2 (page 16) illustrates the dual system in three Australian states. See also Chapter I, note 17, page 102. The English arrangements are briefly summarized below (note 27). It is interesting that in several Australian states there is agitation to use tax money to support in one way or another either private schools or students enrolled in private secondary schools. A comparison of the figures given in Table 2 (page 16) with those given in Table 17 for certain American cities will make it evident that in some localities in the United States we already do have in effect the Australian pattern as far as total private versus public school enrollment is concerned. The difference is the absence in the United States of a *group* of several church-connected schools of approximately equal size all providing four to six years of a college preparatory course.

22. I also find myself on the opposite side of some critics of the public schools who would answer both my questions in the negative. My experience with public school administrators and teachers leads me to conclusions quite different from those who attack the schools as centers for propagating a revolutionary doctrine of a new social order. Yet that the content of education is always open to public debate I quite agree. All charges must be met

by careful examination of the facts. The local community in each case has a right and duty to determine the general type of education to be offered. It is of the utmost importance that the citizens know as much as possible about the local schools. Only on the basis of an enlightened public opinion can the elected school boards operate effectively. (See *Do Citizens and Education Mix? Report of Governor's Fact Finding Commission on Education of Connecticut 1950*; also *Pasadena Faces the Future: A Cooperative Study,* 1952.)

A good example of the settlement of a local controversy by intelligent citizen participation is afforded by the *Report of the Lay Advisory Committee on the Curriculum of the Eugene, Oregon, Public Schools* (issued by authority of the Board of Directors, School District No. 4, Eugene, Oregon, June 25, 1951). In the Foreword it is stated:

"The Lay Advisory Committee to study the curriculum of the Eugene, Oregon, Public Schools was appointed by the school board of District No. 4, Lane County, in April, 1950. Appointment of the committee resulted from criticisms of the school program brought to the attention of the board through petitions requesting that changes be made in the curriculum and methods to provide greater emphasis on the fundamentals.

"After carefully considering the requests made, and discussing them with the leaders of the group which circulated the petitions, the board selected eleven citizens who had children in the schools and who were believed to be representative of various points of view concerning the school program . . ."

The findings and recommendations of this committee that deal with "Social Living" are of particular interest in view of the criticisms leveled at this new type of curriculum in recent years. The committee reports as follows:

"The Social Living or 'core' curriculum has definite strengths. We recognize that knowledge never is in water-tight compartments. Some subjects naturally go together; thus the study of grammar, geography, history, and literature acquires significance when related to the great social movements . . ."

Among the weaknesses found in the program, the committee notes the following:

"1. In the area of public relations. Many parents are suspicious of the very name 'Social Living.' Suddenly they have discovered that vast changes have been made in the past twenty-five years, and they are not sure that they like it. It is human nature to resent the unfamiliar . . .

"6. As this is one class where most children may be reached, there is a tendency to overload the period with extra school activities . . .

"7. There is a lack of 'methodology' for the core studies . . ."

The recommendations of the committee as to the Superior Student are also of special interest, and are as follows:

"That at every level we recognize the responsibility we have to the gifted or able pupil; . . . that at all levels, some effort be made to group such pupils for a limited time each day — enough to provide them with the challenge of competition at their own level, but not sufficient to remove them from the stream of school life."

23. As evidence that in several Protestant denominations there are churchmen with strong attachments to sectarian schools I may cite the following news story printed on April 26, 1952, in *The Pilot* (Boston's official Catholic weekly).

"PROTESTANTS GIVE SUPPORT TO PRIVATE SCHOOL SYSTEM

"Ministerial Assembly Criticizes Dr. Conant

"Protestant spokesmen throughout the United States this week voiced stern opposition and disapproval of charges that private schools are divisive and detrimental to American unity. Their statements reflected the sentiments expressed by Archbishop Cushing in his Easter Sunday warning against the comments of James B. Conant on private schools.

"President Conant of Harvard University called the growth of private schools, including religious schools, a threat to the democratic unity of the United States. Speaking before a national meeting of school administrators in Boston, Dr. Conant said private schools brought a divisive influence in American life and endangered the principle of a single public school system.

"Pastoral Conference

"Members on the New England Pastoral Conference of the Lutheran Church, Missouri Synod, declared on April 23, that they were 'grieved by the indiscriminate attack on religious and private schools precipitated by the recent statement of Harvard's President James B. Conant.' The resolution was passed at a meeting in the Wollaston Lutheran Church. In Chicago this week the National Association of Evangelists, at its annual convention, sprang to the defense of private schools and adopted a resolution urging its constituency to 'protest the tendency toward statism which would threaten the God-given parental right to educate our children.'

"The resolutions of the two gatherings reflected the widespread Protestant resentment of the Harvard President's criticism of the private school system. Numerous ministers throughout the United States expressed similar sentiments in sermons on Sunday, April 20."

As a footnote to this story I might note that I did not use the word "divisive." As in the present chapter, I was speaking *for* the comprehensive high school, not against the private school. Even my sentence, "The greater the proportion of our youth who attend independent schools, the greater the threat to our democratic unity" must be read in connection with the one that immediately follows: "Therefore, to use taxpayers' money to assist such a move is, for me, to suggest that American society use its own hands to destroy itself."

For quotations from churchmen favoring the use of tax money for the support of private schools, see Chapter 6 of V. T. Thayer's *The Attack upon the American Secular School*. In this connection an extremely even-tempered editorial in *The Pilot*, April 12, 1952, is of interest and I give it here in full.

"President Conant this week expressed the wish that the question of a 'dual' system of schools in the United States might be, as he said, 'smoked out.' By a dual system he meant the side by side existence of public schools and those under private auspices, whether parochial or independent. Aside from the fact that the use of the term 'smoked out' rather suggests, and erroneously, that someone has been trying to hide something, the President's sentiments are boldly clear and decidedly against the multiplication of private schools, at least on the secondary level, and in favor of their replacement by 100 percent attendance at public schools, as contrasted with the present 92 percent public school figure.

"In the course of his remarks President Conant suggested that the key questions to be asked for a candid approach to the problem would be two: Should tax funds support private schools? Are private schools divisive in a democratic society? No educator, it seems, should shy away from these questions or assume a position which would require a 'smoking out' process. For our part we feel that the second question should be answered first and let those who feel, as Dr. Conant feels, that the private schools are a threat to our democratic society, bring forth the evidence and allow it to be measured.

"The anti-democratic character of the private (independent, parochial) schools demands serious consideration because if it is genuinely anti-democratic it not only should receive no tax funds or government encouragement but it should in simple truth be destroyed. We simply must not ask that 'American society use its own hands to destroy itself.' The real democratic unity of our country is best served by institutions where, to use Dr. Conant's enumeration, 'the future doctor, lawyer, professor, politician, banker, industrial executive, labor leader, and manual worker' sit down side by side in the same classroom and learn democracy by practising it. We have a suspicion that years ago when President Conant was in Roxbury Latin School (private) he was in the midst of just such a group in spite of the fact that even that school is a somewhat specialized one. We know at least that he could visit (and he would be very welcome) several parochial secondary schools within a few minutes ride of his own University and find young people with ambitions in all the directions he has enumerated, sitting side by side in democratic amiability. We must remind ourselves that most schools separate students within the school itself on lines of ability, vocation, and the like in such a way that, at least in the larger institutions, they manage to have lasting contact only with those whose interests, accomplishments, and plans for the future are quite similar to their own.

"It seems permissible to ask here a somewhat basic question inquiring just how much diversity is desirable. Unity can mean *uniformity*, which suggests imposing a pattern, and until we decide how far along the line we may plant the one without producing the other we might be well advised to pause lest we end up with a single common denominator which may be mediocrity. Many Americans will shrink from a situation which would allow government, local or federal, to control *all* education and will see as the end product a machine easily perverted by the unscrupulous. Long before, and after, the first public school existed in our land, men were being educated for democracy and it would be difficult to demonstrate that theirs was a less virile and vigorous brand.

"Concerning the use of tax funds to assist private or independent schools we may be able to measure the anti-democratic character of this by a reference to the areas in which it is presently practiced: Canada, England, Scotland, Belgium, France, Italy, Netherlands, Germany, Australia and indeed the simple litany of those states which in large measure we now call the democratic West. The 'state-school-alone' program at the same time is being used in those lands farther to the East to impose a unity which is not in any sense democratic.

"We might suggest, then, that the whole question obviously needs more attention than it has up to this time received. Some people with very good intentions are wading in dangerous waters."

Not all church leaders are in favor of the expansion of private schools. For example, the Reverend Frederick M. Meek, Minister of the Old South Church in Boston (Congregational) said on April 29, 1952, at a meeting of the Boston Area Council of Churches:

"We must be strong supporters of the American system of public education. We must resolutely set our faces against the federal support of both private and parochial schools of any creed. If federal support is given to such schools, in the end that support would provide the medium by which the widest variety of schools for educating our children would be established. Little children would be separated from each other on a basis of religious or social or racial or economic status. The result would be the fragmentation of our American Public Education System and when American Public Education is thus fragmented, it would mean the end of our present American democratic system."

I might point out that those of us who oppose the use of tax money for the support of private schools "directly or indirectly" have in mind not only paying the usual costs but such indirect expenses as textbooks and, of course, scholarships. I, for one, however, would not question the tax exemption of property directly used by private schools. The principle of tax exemption of schools, hospitals, and churches seems to be too old and too widely accepted in the United States to be open to debate.

24. In a pamphlet published by The National Union of Christian Schools, for example, it is stated: "Christianity thrives as it permeates all of life more and more. Central in this full program of Kingdom activity is the training of the church's young in such a way that every activity in life shall be a Kingdom activity. This requires a thorough program of daily Christian education. This requires the Christian school. It is in the Christian school and in the Christian school alone that true religion is interrelated with all of life." It would be a fair inference from other statements in this and companion pamphlets that a Catholic parochial school would not meet the requirements of this group as a "Christian school" for their children. For those who hold such views the Australian or English pattern would seem to represent the ideal pattern.

There is nothing new about sectarian hostility to public schools. A biographer of Horace Mann, writing for the *Dictionary of American Biography* published in 1933, states that this educational reformer's efforts aroused bitter opposition. "As a Unitarian he contended that the Bible should be read in public schools, but without comment. He had scarcely entered upon his progressive educational program when one church after another began to charge him and the board of education with being responsible for creating a godless system of schools. With these charges came the demand that sectarian instruction, which had been excluded . . . by an act of 1827 should be restored. Mann met these sectarian attacks with vigor, courage, and a final victory of great importance not only to the schools of Massachusetts, but to the nation at large."

The use of the word "final" in the last sentence by the author of this biographical note is of interest. One hopes that the events of the next fifty years will not prove that he was wrong. The charge that public schools, being nonsectarian, are "godless" is at least a century old. What is new in recent years is the religious dogmatism of certain groups which has made impossible even the reading of the Bible without comment in the public schools of some states and localities. Yet it is from the same groups that come spokesmen from time to time to attack the public schools for being "godless."

25. *Pierce, Governor of Oregon et al.* v. *Society of Sisters*; and *Pierce, Governor of Oregon et al.* v. *Hill Military Academy* (268 U.S. 510–536) 1925.

26. John Stuart Mill's remarks on education and the state are sometimes quoted by the proponents of private schools. There can be no doubt about Mill's position. If his views had prevailed there would be no public schools in the American sense anywhere in the British Commonwealth. He wrote his famous essay on "Liberty" in which he expressed his fears of state schools in 1856. At that time both secondary and primary education in England were in the hands of voluntary organizations (Chapter I, note 7, page 93). With this in mind, and remembering that Mill was an agnostic living in a nation with an established church, the following extract from the essay on "Liberty" can be read with understanding; it reflects the outlook of an important section of the governing class of England in the second half of the nineteenth century which feared that through state schools the Church of England would once again attempt to destroy the nonconformists. (See note 29, page 151, below.)

"Is it not almost a self-evident axiom, that the State should require and compel the education, up to a certain standard, of every human being who is born its citizen? Yet who is there that is not afraid to recognize and assert this truth? . . .

"Were the duty of enforcing universal education once admitted, there would be an end to the difficulties about what the State should teach, and how it should teach, which now convert the subject into a mere battle field for sects and parties, causing the time and labor which should have been spent in educating, to be wasted in quarrelling about education. If the government would make up its mind to require for every child a good education, it might save itself the trouble of providing one. It might leave to parents to obtain the education where and how they pleased, and content itself with helping to pay the school fees of the poorer classes of children, and defraying the entire school expenses of those who have no one else to pay for them. The objections which are argued with reason against State education, do not apply to the enforcement of education by the State, but to the State's taking upon itself to direct that education; which is a totally different thing. That the whole or any large part of the education of the people should be in State hands, I go as far as any one in deprecating. All that has been said of the importance of individuality of character, and diversity in opinions and modes of conduct, involves, as of the same unspeakable importance, diversity of education. A general State education is a mere contrivance for moulding people to be exactly like one another: and as the mould in which it casts them is that which pleases the predominant power in the government, whether this be a monarch, a priesthood, an aristocracy, or the majority of the existing generation; in proportion as it is efficient and successful, it establishes a despotism over the mind, leading by natural tendency to one over the body. An education established and controlled by the State should only exist, if it exist at all, as one among many competing experiments, carried on for the purpose of example and stimulus, to keep the others up to a certain standard of excellence. Unless, indeed, when society in general is in so backward a state that it could or would not provide for itself any proper institutions of education, unless the government undertook the task: then, indeed, the government may, as the less of two great evils, take upon itself the business of schools and universities, as it may that of joint stock-companies, when private enterprise, in a shape fitted for undertaking great works of industry, does not exist in the country. But in general, if the country contains a sufficient number of persons qualified to provide education under government auspices, the same persons would be able and willing to give an equally good education on the voluntary principle, under the assurance of remuneration afforded by a law rendering education compulsory, combined with State aid to those unable to defray the expense.

"The instrument for enforcing the law could be no other than public examinations, extending to all children, and beginning at an early age. An age might be fixed at which every child must be examined, to ascertain if he (or she) is able to read. If a child proves unable, the father, unless he has some sufficient ground of excuse, might be subjected to a moderate fine, to be worked out, if necessary, by his labor, and the child might be put to school at his expense. Once in every year the examination should be renewed, with a gradually extending range of subjects, so as to make the universal acquisition, and what is more, retention, of a certain minimum of general knowledge, virtually compulsory. Beyond that minimum, there should be voluntary examinations on all subjects, at which all who come up to a certain standard of proficiency might claim a certificate. To prevent the State from exercising, through these arrangements, an improper influence over opinion, the knowledge required for passing an examination (beyond the merely instrumental parts of knowledge, such as languages and their use) should, even in the higher classes of examinations, be confined to facts and positive science exclusively. The examinations on religion, politics, or other disputed topics, should not turn on the truth or falsehood of opinions, but on the matter of fact that such and such an opinion is held, on such grounds, by such authors, or schools, or churches. Under this system, the rising generation would be no worse off in regard to all disputed truths, than they are at present; they would be brought up either churchmen or dissenters as they now are, the State merely taking care that they should be instructed churchmen, or instructed dissenters. There would be nothing to hinder them from being taught religion, if their parents chose, at the same schools where they were taught other things. *All attempts by the State to bias the conclusions of its citizens on disputed subjects are evil;* but it may very properly offer to ascertain and certify that a person possesses the knowledge requisite to make his conclusions, on any given subject, worth attending to. . ." (italics mine). J. S. Mill, *On Liberty and Considerations on Representative Government* (Oxford: Basil Blackwell, 1948), pp. 94–97.

Mill's views are in striking contrast to those of Jefferson or the American educational leaders of the first half of the nineteenth century (Barnard or Mann, for example) who firmly established the free public school in so many states. The cleavage between the English and the American outlook on education is more than a century old. From the point of view of those who believe in universal education for *all* the youth of a nation, England is only now beginning to develop an adequate system of schools. It might be said not unfairly that one of the main reasons why Great Britain has been so backward in developing education is that Mill's fears were shared by so many influential citizens.

Mill's emphasis on examinations and knowledge certified by public authorities again reflects influential British opinion of a century ago. The significance of this emphasis on the state control of education through examinations has been commented on in Chapters I and II.

27. The place of religious instruction in the schools of England as a consequence of the Act of 1944 is of special interest to all concerned with the public support of private schools. The present situation is briefly as follows: In addition to schools maintained and managed entirely by public authorities (the county councils) there are a number of private schools that in one way or another receive public funds. As explained earlier (Chapter I, note 7, page 93), these schools may receive direct grants, or be "aided" or "controlled" schools. In the first two cases the religious instruction may be as exclusively denominational as the trustees may desire, but at least half the costs of upkeep of the buildings must be met by the trustees. In the "controlled schools" all financial obligations are assumed by the local educational authorities though the ownership of the property remains in the hands of the trustees (p. 94). Denominational instruction may be given for not more than two periods a week to the children whose parents desire it. "Apart from such denominational teaching, the religious instruction must be in accordance with an agreed syllabus. . . . The syllabus is decided locally by means of a conference called by the local education authority and consisting of representatives of the religious denominations concerned, the teacher's associations and the authority." (*A Guide to the Educational System of England and Wales*, Ministry of Education Pamphlet No. 2, London, 1945, p. 26 and footnote.)

The Act of 1944 requires that "the school day in every county school and in every voluntary school shall begin with collective worship on the part of all pupils in attendance at the school" and that "religious instruction shall be given in every county school and in every voluntary school." There is a provision, however, which safeguards the rights of a parent who requests that his child may be excused from attendance at religious worship or religious instruction. An "agreed syllabus" for religious instruction is used not only in the "controlled" private schools but in the county schools (public schools in the American sense). (The independent schools which receive no public money do not fall within these provisions of the Act of 1944.)

The official statement of the Ministry of Education summarizes the situation as follows: "The result of these provisions of the Act is not only to make available the financial assistance needed by the voluntary schools [that is, private schools] to enable their premises to be brought up to modern standards and enable these schools to play a full and effective part in the primary and secondary school system, but also to ensure that they retain liberty for the teaching of the tenets of the Church with which they are associated by teachers of their own faith. The appointment of teachers in controlled schools by the local education authority reduces the field of religious tests for teachers, while the provision of agreed syllabus religious instruction in controlled schools and, when necessary in aided schools, meets the needs of parents of other faiths in areas which are served by a single voluntary school." (A Guide to the Educational System of England and Wales, p. 27, sec. 88.)

Church of England schools are today either independent (the "Public Schools"), direct grant, controlled, or aided. The Roman Catholic schools are either independent, direct grant, or aided. Of 168 direct-grant schools only 72 are under church control (54 Roman Catholic, some 10 Anglican). In 1950 there were, according to the Annual Report of the Minister of Education, 271 Church of England secondary schools, 186 Roman Catholic, and 314 of other denominations out of a total of 4,765 secondary schools maintained at public expense (controlled or aided). While the total number of children attending denominational schools in England is not large, for those in school full time at age 17 the percentage attending schools other than county schools is high (over 60 per cent). Of these about one third are enrolled in either direct-grant or maintained voluntary schools (Chapter I, note 7, page 93). One may estimate that perhaps some 10 or 15 per cent of boys 17 years of age attending school were enrolled in denominational schools supported largely by tax money. In a few localities, at least, the percentage of the boys still in school at 17 who were in one or more church-connected schools might be as high as 50 or 60 per cent. In a few towns there may be as many as three different denominational secondary schools receiving public funds.

To an American, the Act of 1944 would seem to have gone a very long way indeed down the road of complete support of denominational schools by tax money. Yet neither the Roman Catholic Church nor the Anglican Church seems entirely satisfied. This is brought out by some remarks by a prominent Catholic layman and the Archbishop of Canterbury in a recent debate in the House of Lords (March 19, 1952). (Parliamentary Debates [Hansard], House of Lords Official Report, Vol. 175, No. 38, pp. 804–805.) In the course of a speech dealing with various phases of education, Lord Pakenham (Labor) had this to say about religious instruction:

"I should now like to come to the question of religious education. There must be many noble Lords — perhaps the majority of the House, but perhaps not — who agree with me in thinking that religious education is the most important part of education — I would say, indeed, far the most important part of education. It seems to me that that is a conclusion which is reached by the majority of practising Christians and practising members of all the great religions, including the Jewish community in this country and elsewhere. . . .

"I would submit, further, with, I believe, a considerable degree of acceptance, that religious education in school is not merely a matter of teaching one particular subject, whether it is called divinity or scripture, or whatever else. It is a question of the ethos, the whole atmosphere in the schools, which in the case certainly of Christian children should, surely, be that of a believing child, coming from a home of believers and taught in a school by Christian believers. I would go further — because what I have just said seems to be a religious right — and say that, politically speaking, there is the right of all Christian citizens, as rate-payers or taxpayers, to be guaranteed a situation where the State does not discriminate against them."

This last sentence of Lord Pakenham is of considerable significance as stating what might be called the English position on religious education, namely, that unless tax money flows as freely to all denominational schools as to other schools there is a curtailment of freedom of religion. To most Americans this argument is so foreign as to be amazing. Lord Pakenham then continued:

"I cannot accept for a moment the argument that religion is a sort of gadget or an idiosyncrasy for which people ought to pay extra, as though they suddenly wanted to learn Russian or some subject which might be useful but was really quite eccentric as a demand from the average child. May I say, with all humility, that it is a great source of gratification that the most reverend Primate the Archbishop of Canterbury is going to address us later on behalf of the Church of England? I have no claims to speak on behalf of anybody. Though I myself am a Roman Catholic, I do not speak on behalf of that Church. We shall, of course, listen with the greatest deference to the most reverend Primate. . . .

". . . how far is it true today that Roman Catholic children have equal educational opportunity with the majority of their fellows? The position is broadly determined by the Act of 1944. I do not want to rake up any embers of past controversy, but I am one who regards that Act as not doing justice to denominational education, whether Roman Catholic or other. It seems to me an historic Act, and in many respects an Act of statesmanship; but it left a great deal that could have been desired. Apart from its abstract merits or demerits, which we could debate at considerable length, it has left behind it an unhappy aftermath in two respects that were not foreseen by anybody at that time, and certainly not by the authors of the Act. In the first place, building costs have continued to rise far beyond any expectations formed in 1944. . . . So in 1950 we reached the position — I do not think it has altered much since, one way or the other — that the Government and the Roman Catholic hierarchy were in broad agreement that the total bill facing the Roman Catholic community over a period of years amounted to over £50,000,000, which I am sure it is fair to say is vastly more than anybody expected in 1944 — perhaps it is three times as great, perhaps rather more than that. That is the position; and I am trying to test the application of the principle acceptable to most of us, that there should be no discrimination, against the fact.

"Other religious communions — and I say this in no spirit of envy, but as a fact — are able in conscience to accept agreed syllabus religious instruction, supplemented within the terms of the 1944 Act. No doubt the Archbishop will tell us more about the Church of England position this afternoon. As a result, where that can be accepted, those communions can have the cost of their children's education defrayed entirely out of public funds [that is, the schools are controlled rather than aided]. I am not saying that they like it in every case, but I leave it to the Archbishop to express their attitude. Catholics, on the other hand, are unable in conscience to accept a compromise of that sort, and therefore they have to meet this very heavy financial outlay [that is, half the building expenses]."

In reply the Archbishop of Canterbury said in part:

"I came here to-day because the noble Lord, Lord Pakenham, kindly told me that he was going to refer to religious education . . . If I had known what the noble Lord was going to say, I should not have come, because all that he said about religious education I entirely support, and I agree with every word he said, too, on administrative questions, although I shall have something to say on that matter in a moment. Even though the noble Lord did not deliver such a ferocious attack on the 1944 Act as I expected, I may be allowed to remind your Lordships what the general attitude of the Church of England to that 1944 Act was, because, whatever adjustments are made to it, I think it is important to remember what has gone before. The first point I would make about the reasons why the Church of England accepted the 1944 Act is this: that it was the first Education Act in the history of this country which was not the subject of bitter inter-denominational strife and struggle. . . ."

Lord Pakenham: "I will not interrupt the most reverend Primate further except to say that the settlement was never accepted by the Catholic hierarchy. That was the point I felt it right to insist upon at this stage."

The Lord Archbishop of Canterbury: "That is what I have said and I am going to say again: no Church was satisfied with that solution — not a single one of them. The Roman Catholic Church, as I was going to say, openly expressed its dissatisfaction, and the Roman hierarchy said that they could not accept it. The Church of England said frankly that this was not all that they desired. They hoped that, as things developed and the area of conflict and controversy faded, a better settlement would be possible, and that the Church of England would be given more of what it desired. I want to make it perfectly clear that the Church of England was not satisfied. I think the Free Churches also were not satisfied, in this sense: that if the Roman Catholic Church, the Free Churches and the Church of England had each drafted the Bill themselves, the Bill would have been very different indeed from the Act which was finally passed. That is what I want to underline: that the Bill was accepted as a result of people in general feeling: 'While this is not what we want, it is the most that can be got without reopening the whole field of internecine conflict and passionate controversy.' The Church of England has from that day to this declared that in its view the time is not ripe to disturb the principle of the

1944 Act, for this reason: that, so far as they can see, there is no likelihood of reaching a greater area of agreement now than there was in 1944. The present position of this country is not one in which we want to have our attention distracted by a bitter educational and religious controversy. So our position is — and we have declared it again and again — that, unsatisfactory in many ways though the 1944 Act was, when it was accepted as the best we could secure at that moment, we do not think that the position is such that the principle could be re-opened now without grave crisis. . . .

"As your Lordships will remember, the 1944 Act made religious worship and teaching compulsory in every school, primary and secondary. It became a necessary part of the State's provision of education. I would say that that is a triumph for the Christian cause. It does mean at least that every child going through the schools of the nation is brought into some kind of confrontation with the Scriptures, with the Revelation therein contained and the powers of Christian faith. The alternative to that is further secularism, in which in the schools of the country there is no religious teaching at all. As your Lordships know well, that is the system which exists in the United States of America. As between these two, there is no kind of doubt that any Christian would choose the solution of the Act of 1944."

The last remark of the Archbishop points up more clearly than I can the antithesis between the American and the English pattern of education. The question before the American public in the second half of the twentieth century is: do we wish to shift from the one to the other?

28. As in England, public money is used in Scotland for the support of a certain number of private schools (see Chapter I, note 14, page 99). These include Roman Catholic and Episcopal schools. However, this is not the usual procedure for providing for the religious instruction in denominational schools. The religious history of Scotland from the Reformation on has been so different from that of England that it is not surprising to find great differences in the relation of the churches to the tax-supported schools. The deep cleavage between the Dissenters (Nonconformists) and the Church of England which has affected so many aspects of English history has no parallel north of the border. Therefore the fear of state schools expressed, for example, by John Stuart Mill (p. 144) seems never to have infected Scottish thinking. The present system of education in the Northern Kingdom can be regarded as an extension of the arrangement set up by the Act of the British Parliament in 1872. Writing in 1878 of the results of this Act, one of Her Majesty's Inspectors of Schools reported as follows:

"The effect of the Act on the Roman Catholic and Episcopal schools has been, if anything, to give a fresh impulse to their extension. They are now the only existing Church schools pure and simple, but it must not be supposed that they are the solitary remnants of denominationalism. In point of fact, the machinery by which our national system is worked is mostly denominational. . . .

"The boards, with surprising uniformity of action, or rather inaction, practically left the subject [that is, religious instruction] in the position in which they found it. They settled it everywhere and in every case on its traditional basis. They simply stereotyped and enforced the hereditary *status quo,* or what is termed 'use and wont.' The mass of the Scotch people are Presbyterians, and for these the national schools may be said to exist, just as the Roman Catholic and Episcopal schools respectively exist for these denominations. The public schools are to all intents and purposes denominational schools. *Public and Presbyterian are practically interchangeable terms* [italics mine]. Inspection is, perhaps, after all the only really undenominational feature in our educational arrangements. But the system is said to work well. Everybody is pleased, and the religious difficulty is solved." (Report of Scottish Education Department, 1878–1879, p. 173, as quoted in *Memorandum with Regard to the Provision Made for Religious Instruction in the Schools in Scotland,* Scottish Education Department, Edinburgh, 1943, reprinted 1949, p. 6.)

Schools other than public schools (in the American and Scottish sense of the word "public") were left free by the Act of 1872 to continue under voluntary management, and they might receive Government grants. This arrangement was continued by the Act of 1918 and there are now fifteen grant-aided secondary schools. However, only a few per cent of the total school population of Scotland is enrolled in grant-aided schools.

The Act of 1918 provided that voluntary schools might be transferred to the local Education Authority (see Chapter I, note 14, page 99) with certain safeguards for the continuation of denominational religious instruction. Such transferred schools might be said to be under joint control, since for all secular instruction they are under the management of the Education Authority (which owns the property and pays all the bills). The continuance of the denominational nature of the schools is insured, however, by (a) a guarantee that the time set apart for religious instruction will not be less than before the transfer; (b) the appointment of only teachers approved "as regards religious belief and character by representatives of the Church or denominational body concerned"; (c) the appointment of a supervisor of religious instruction approved by the Church or denominational body. More than 300 private (voluntary) schools have been transferred under this act; 226 Roman Catholic schools, 50 Episcopal schools, 3 Church of Scotland schools, one United Free Church school, 21 unclassified. The Act of 1918 also provided for the building of new schools by the local Education Authority to be held under the same conditions as transferred schools. Eighteen new Roman Catholic schools, and one Episcopal school have been thus established.

The following quotation from the official *Memorandum* of the Scottish Education Department of 1943 describes the provisions for "Secondary Education for Roman Catholic and Episcopalian Children":

"Secondary education is provided in Roman Catholic and Episcopal schools where the demand is sufficient to justify such special provision. Secondary education is of two types — junior, providing a three-year course suitable for pupils between the ages of 12 and 15, and senior, providing a five or six year course suitable for pupils between the ages of 12 and 17 or 18. The time devoted to religious instruction varies, but is usually from three to four hours a week. In most cases the junior secondary instruction is given to Roman Catholic and Episcopalian children in the same building as the primary instruction, although in areas such as Aberdeen, Dundee,

Edinburgh, Glasgow, Dunbartonshire, Lanarkshire, and Renfrewshire, where
there is a considerable Roman Catholic population of school age, the Roman
Catholic junior secondary pupils from certain transferred schools have
been centralised in separate Roman Catholic schools. So far as senior
secondary education is concerned, there are 20 Roman Catholic secondary
schools conducted by the Education Authorities of Dundee, Edinburgh,
Glasgow, Ayrshire, Dunbartonshire, Fife, Lanarkshire, Renfrewshire,
Stirlingshire, and West Lothian, and two Roman Catholic voluntary secondary schools, one in Aberdeen and one in Glasgow. In the other areas there are
no Roman Catholic secondary schools, and in no area is there an Episcopal
secondary school: Roman Catholic and Episcopalian children wishing to
receive secondary education proceed to the ordinary secondary schools, and
are taught there, subject to the right to withdraw from the religious instruction as provided in the Conscience Clause. Where, however, there is a
sufficient number of Roman Catholic or Episcopalian children, special provision is sometimes made for their religious instruction." The Scottish pattern
is thus clearly different from the American, Australian, or English.

29. The religious provisions of the Act of 1944 cannot be fully understood without some knowledge of the history of English education. The
requirement of religious education in terms of an "agreed syllabus" for all
but direct-grant and aided schools (with the right of withdrawal of
children by parents) at first sight seems a sensible arrangement that should
satisfy all religious groups. But the debate in the House of Lords quoted in
note 27 makes evident that it does not. One can hardly expect the churchmen
of several denominations to accept any such compromise unless *full* public
support of strictly denominational schools is likewise included. This is the
direction in which England has been moving for fifty years.

In the brief description of the English system given on page 93 (Chapter I,
note 7), attention was called to the fact that in 1902 by Act of Parliament,
public money was used for the maintenance of certain denominational schools.
This Act was passed only after heated debate on the issue of using tax money
for religious schools. Writing of this period, S. J. Curtis in his *History of Education in Great Britain* (London, 1948) says (pp. 320–321): "The Liberals
[who had opposed the Act] were not content to acknowledge defeat . . .
Many Nonconformists refused to pay their rates and distraint was made on
their property . . .

". . . When the election of 1906 was fought, the Liberals included
the repeal of the Education Act of 1902 . . . as part of their political
programme. The result of the election was a great landslide in favour of the
Liberals . . . Within a few months, Mr. Birrell [President of the Board of
Education] presented a Bill to Parliament which was designed to meet
the grievances of the Nonconformists. One of its principal clauses proposed
the abolition of the voluntary schools by transferring them to the Local Educational Authorities. After a stormy debate the Bill went to the Lords, where
it was amended so drastically that the Government refused to proceed any
further with it.

"Dr. Clifford wanted to force a constitutional issue with the Lords —
to mend or end the House — but the Act had now been working with great
success for four years and the Government thought it unwise to follow this

line of action. A further attempt to reverse the 1902 policy was made by Mr. McKenna, who was president of the Board in 1908. His proposals did not satisfy the Nonconformists and roused the intense opposition of the Anglicans and Roman Catholics. . . . Yet another attempt at reversal was made in the same year by Mr. Runciman . . . , but the combined opposition of the Church, the Roman Catholics and this time the teachers . . . convinced him that it would be wise to withdraw his Bill. By this time Mr. Runciman and the Government realized that the Education Act of 1902 had come to stay."

The Act of 1902 dealt almost entirely with elementary education; there was little or no provision for support of secondary education. But the principle was established that public funds were to be used for meeting the costs of instruction in denominational schools which provided the school buildings and met the expenses of the upkeep of these buildings. The Act of 1944 carried this principle over into the field of secondary education and broadened the uses to which public funds were used by including the full costs of alterations and improvements in the buildings for "controlled" schools and half the same costs for aided schools. The next step for which Lord Pakenham appears to be arguing (note 27, p. 147) would be the payment of full costs for buildings as well as instruction for the aided schools, or in other words the elimination altogether of the category of controlled schools.

30. *General Education in Transition*, edited by N. T. Morse (University of Minnesota Press, Minneapolis, 1951), Chapter VI, "General Education and Specialism in British Universities," by T. R. McConnell.

31. A. V. Heely, *Why the Private School?* (Harper Bros., New York, 1951) is a vigorous statement, by the Headmaster of the Lawrenceville School, on behalf of the nondenominational private school. Recognizing the difficulties of patronizing a private school and supporting public schools (both of which he recommends), he writes (p. 20):

"Much harm is also done to the cause of unity by the failure of patrons of the private schools to concern themselves with the quality of their local public schools. I have often heard parents say that they were compelled to send their children to school away from home because the local public schools were inferior. [One might interrupt Mr. Heely by wondering if his experience has not been similar to mine in encountering parents who really had in mind social considerations, not intellectual stimulation or pedagogic efficiency, when they preferred a private school. Yet in giving a reason they felt obliged to condemn the local public school as an inferior school, though without much evidence.] But I do not have the impression that they were disturbed about them, as they should have been, let alone that they were engaged in working for their improvement. I have even known parents to oppose a raise in the tax rate, intended to improve the quality of local public schools, who at the same time were sending their children to expensive private schools. All this makes for bitterness and antagonism to everybody's hurt."

On page 58 Mr. Heely writes: "If it is agreed that the independent school has a national function to perform . . . it seems essential that federal scholarships be provided to support its program." I find myself among those who are strongly opposed to federal or state scholarships for those attending private secondary schools. Such scholarships must be, after all, only a device for supporting private secondary schools with public money. It is because of the dangers in this direction that I must disagree with those who insist that the independent school has a national function apart from its role as a means of supplementing public education when the latter is not yet adequate.

Mr. Heely is not defeatist in his attitude towards the possibility of the public schools' doing a good job for the gifted boy or girl. But some educators are. President John W. Nason of Swarthmore College, speaking at Exeter Academy on May 24, 1952, said: "For the majority of high school students secondary education is terminal, and we cannot reasonably ask the public schools to concentrate on the minority of students preparing for college." What many of us are doing is to ask for more concentration on this minority; the alternative would seem to be to have only gifted boys of the higher income brackets adequately prepared for college and professional training.

32. A highly important step in the direction of providing a greater degree of local control for schools in a large city was taken recently in New York. If successful, it will warrant being copied in other metropolitan areas. Under the title "Local Autonomy in a City School System," J. O. Loretan, Assistant Superintendent of Schools in New York City, describes, in a memorandum dated June 1952, the Bronx Park Community Project. A community of 140,000 people living within an area of about four square miles is served by ten elementary schools and one high school. Under a charter provided by the Superintendent of Schools, this community has now elected a nine-member school committee to act as an advisory body to the New York City officials in charge of the schools in this community. The advantages of a decentralization of a vast city school system in terms of citizen understanding and responsibility are obvious. To what degree administrative control can be delegated to autonomous boards within a city framework is a matter for the future to determine. But unless some such arrangements as those now in force in the Bronx Park Community can be achieved, our large cities cannot benefit from the type of citizen participation which was so successful in Eugene, Oregon (note 22, above).

33. *Moral and Spiritual Values in the Public Schools*, Educational Policies Commission (Washington, D. C., 1951). This volume opens with the following statement:

"A great and continuing purpose of education has been the development of moral and spiritual values. To fulfill this purpose, society calls upon all its institutions. Special claims are made on the home and the school because of the central role of these two institutions in the nurture of the young.

"By moral and spiritual values we mean those values which, when applied in human behavior, exalt and refine life and bring it into accord with the standards of conduct that are approved in our democratic culture.

"The American people have rightly expected the schools of this country to teach moral and spiritual values. The schools have accepted this responsibility. . . ."

A few paragraphs later it is pointed out that "As public institutions, the public schools of this nation must be non-denominational. They can have no part in securing acceptance of any one of the numerous systems of belief regarding a supernatural power and the relation of mankind thereto." The second and third chapters of this one-hundred-page book are devoted to the analysis of the values that the American people are agreed on and how various sanctions for right conduct can be illustrated in a school situation.

Anyone who is disturbed by the charges that our public schools are "godless" or antireligious should read this little volume (particularly the program in Chapter IV) and see to what extent he or she agrees with its objectives. What many people fail to realize is that the elimination of collective worship and Bible reading from many public schools has not been the result of atheistic or agnostic propaganda. It has been a consequence of the fundamental incompatibility of the religious doctrines of Catholics, Protestants, and Jews. The religious syllabus agreed upon in England (note 27, above) was possible only *after* state funds had been made available to Anglican and Roman Catholic secondary schools.

34. In a pamphlet (now out of print) entitled *Federal-State Relations in Education*, published jointly by the Educational Policies Commission and the Problems and Policies Committee of the American Council on Education in March 1945, the summary (page 44) starts with these words: "The purpose of this statement is to warn the American people of an ominous trend toward the federalizing of education in the United States and to propose policies and procedures by which citizens may resist and reverse this dangerous trend."

What the writers of this document had in mind in 1945 particularly is evident from the description on page 8 of what had occurred in the depression years. "The National Youth Administration was the farthest advance of the federal government into the field of educational control during the depression . . . In the N.Y.A. the national government set up its own organization for the direct administration of youth education. . . . The NYA began to establish schools of its own in direct competition with established public school systems. The youths who attended these schools were paid from federal funds. . . ."

The concluding two paragraphs of this pamphlet read as follows:

"The United States Government needs a clear-cut policy to define its relations to education. The chief elements of such a policy are (1) federal grants to assure an adequate financial basis for education everywhere in the nation, (2) distribution of the federal grants on an objective basis which leaves the control of educational processes to the states and localities, and (3) well-organized federal advisory and informational services and leadership concerning education. Such a policy would provide the educational program that this nation must have for its own safety and for the well-being of its citizens.

"Unfortunately, such a policy has not been adopted or implemented at the present time. The present situation is one of drift toward an increasing control over education by the federal government, exhibited in some cases by actual operation of educational programs from Washington. The drift in this direction has been accelerating in recent years. Our democratic technical society requires an abundance of good education. In the long run, the best way to provide that education is under a decentralized pattern of educational organization which keeps the schools close to the people and responsive to their needs and wishes."

One who reads these paragraphs written seven years ago must agree that while no clear-cut policy of the Federal Government has been developed, nevertheless, there has been little or no increase in the actual operation of educational programs from Washington. There has been no need for any successor to the N.Y.A., but we may well be on our guard if another depression should occur. If the public schools are strong, there will be little reason for a Federal program.

INDEX

INDEX

A.B. degree, 43

Academic high schools, New Zealand, 48

Academic training in languages and mathematics, 57

Academically able youth, identifying, 64

Academies (U.S.), 27

Act of 1872 (Parliament), establishing elementary education for Scotland, 12

Act of 1944 (Parliament), 7, 93, 145; financial and administrative arrangements under, 96; county colleges envisaged by, 120

Adelaide, South Australia, private schools, 16

Adelaide, University of, 126

Adolescents, educational patterns, 3. *See also* Secondary Education

Advisory Council on Education in Scotland, 100

Agricultural and mechanical arts colleges, 44

"Aided School," 94

America, relation of education to remunerative work, 44. *See also* United States

American Association of School Administrators, ix

American bachelor's degree in science, standard of, 121

American college, the, 29–54; as special phenomenon, 31, 34; origin of, 34–39; expansion of, 42–45; demand for liberal education, 43; future of, 56

American democracy, basic tenets of, 56

American liberal arts college, no equivalent in England of, 15; success of, 55

American pattern of education,

uniqueness of, 2, 4–5; contrast with English, 10; characteristics of, 24, 46; eventual shift in, 58; continuance of, 78. *See also* United States

American schools and colleges, program for future of, 56–60

American Secular School, The Attack upon (V. T. Thayer), 140

American tradition of local responsibility, 26

Anglo-American Council on Productivity, *Productivity Report on the Universities and Industry*, 121

Anglo-Saxon education, influence of Scotland on, 12

Anglo-Saxon tradition, in secondary education, 1–28

Antagonistic cultural groups, 63

Antioch College, 135

Apprentice training, British system of, 75

Archbishop of Canterbury, 146

Arnold of Rugby, 33

Attack upon the American Secular School, The (V. T. Thayer), 140

Auckland University College, 124

Australia, pattern of secondary education, 2, 3, 12–13, 16–20, 78; compared with U.S., 4; dual system, 16; Protestant private schools, compared with New Zealand, 23; educational patterns of university and college students, 30, 69; tax-supported secondary schools, 48; technical schools and colleges, 75; religious composition of the population, 108; external examinations, 122–123; matriculation requirements in universities, 126

Australian Commonwealth Scholarships, 132

Australian independent school, the, 16